Published in 2006 by
Herridge & Sons Ltd
Lower Forda, Shebbear
Devon EX21 5SY

Design by Ray Leaning

ISBN 0-9549981-2-X
Printed in China

CONTENTS

INTRODUCTION

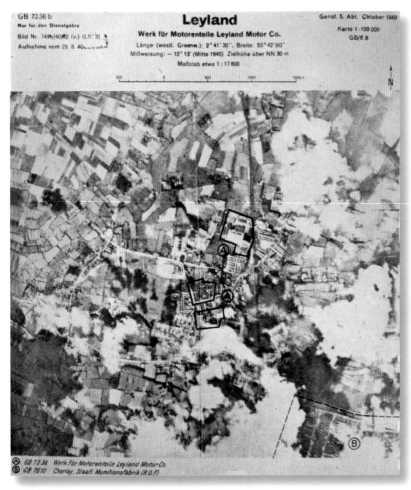

When I came across the collection of commercial vehicle sales material which I have used as a basis for this book the first thing that came to me was that here was a story told by the participants themselves.

Great Britain in 1945 was severely battered, despite having emerged victorious from nearly six years of war. Its motor manufacturers had been called upon to produce huge quantities of the most diverse products, often under the most difficult conditions. They had responded magnificently, but there was still much to be done with the task of postwar reconstruction, both at home and abroad. Export markets were once again opening up and export was going to be essential in order to refill the nation's depleted coffers.

Those makers who had developed specialised vehicles for carrying heavy equipment and for use on difficult terrain were in a relatively good position as these could be civilianised and would find a ready market abroad, from forestry in South America to oilfields in the Middle East. Other manufacturers, however, had simply produced militarised versions of their 1930s products or even, in some cases, suspended vehicle production altogether for the duration. Either way, in order to get back into the market quickly, these firms had little alternative other than to recommence manufacture of their existing designs with, in some cases a little hasty revamping.

It was in these difficult years of the late 1940s,

A German aerial photograph of Leyland, captured from the Luftwaffe, on which the company's factories are clearly marked as target A.

A Leyland Retriever searchlight lorry. The 'light', just unloaded, will be connected to an onboard 24kw generator driven from the auxiliary gearbox. Retrievers were also built to perform a multiplicity of other roles from breakdown to mobile workshop.

which on the one hand offered so much but on the other placed sometimes almost insurmountable strictures on industry, that some of the old established manufacturers began to fall prey to their rivals. This process was irreversible and, in common with the rest of Britain's motor industry, the resulting erosion of individuality coupled with other forces has culminated today in extinction or absorption for almost all. Those that did survive those years began, hesitantly at first, to come up with vehicles that would fulfil the changing needs of the haulage industry and at the same time reflect people's growing awareness of fashion. Some attempts at the latter are pretty horrid in retrospect whilst others have grown old gracefully.

This book traces the paths that manufacturers took during the first 20 years after the war, from immediate postwar austerity to the swinging sixties. This period saw immense change: from commercials which were barely able to reach 30mph (let alone allowed by law to exceed it) to the dawning of the motorway age which promised so much; from the cloth cap image of the 1940s to the emancipated trucker of the '60s.

This book is not intended to be encyclopaedic and there will be makes and models which are absent, but I believe you will find the majority well represented. The brochures and catalogues which I have drawn upon range from the crude and unat-tractive to others with inspired artwork or slick presentation. They are however the means that the manufactures used to sell their products – warts, wrinkles and all.

The majority of the material reproduced here is drawn from the collection of my late friend Peter Richley, with some gaps filled by the kind loan of further material by James Horn.

Rinsey Mills
October 2005

"I'd give something to be riding down Deansgate!"

SUPPLY driver today— transport operator tomorrow? He has driven Morris-Commercials in the heat and sand. He knows the quality of their workmanship and performance. He asks for nothing better than to own one after the war. Morris-Commercials always had a good name, but this war has proved it up to the tail-board. You live and learn . . .

MORRIS-COMMERCIAL

AEC

The streets of London, during the first few years of the 20th century, underwent a total transformation as horse drawn transport was replaced by the motor vehicle. In control of public transport services throughout the capital since the 1850s was the London General Omnibus Company, and in 1910 they began to produce motor buses of their own. Two years later the LGOC was bought by the owners of London's vast underground railway system, who immediately set up a separate company to manufacture buses. This they called the Associ-ated Equipment Company and, as it was under the aegis of the London Underground, it took the familiar motif of that organisation and simply substituted the initials AEC for the word 'underground'.

AEC continued production of the LGOC B type bus, which on the battlefields of the First World War became a legend as a troop carrier. During 1916, using the first moving assembly line in Europe, the company started to turn out large numbers of its ¾-ton lorry on the newly designed Y type chassis for use both at the front and in general military service.

As a result of this, once the war was over, AEC found itself with a production line and workforce capable of producing far more commercials than were required by its parent company, and consequently its products became available to the general public. During the early 1920s the majority of both buses and lorries – the wartime Y type now with increased payload and known as the 501 - were sold within the environs of London, and in order to try and enlarge the sales sphere a liaison with Daimler was entered into around 1927. A year later the company moved out of the East End to a much larger site at Southall in Middlesex and shortly after ended its ties with Daimler. The larger factory signalled increased production and the development of new models, and it was there, in 1930, that the company began to produce what was almost certainly the first diesel engine to be built by an English commercial vehicle manufacturer.

Shortly afterwards a new range of trucks began to roll off the production line, some of them given names that were to remain synonymous with the marque, such as the Monarch and Mammoth. During 1933, with a reorganisation of the manner in which London's public transport was administered, the Underground companies became a part of the London Passenger Transport Board, with the exception of AEC, which henceforth struck out on its own as a totally separate entity.

Although the firm was still best known for its buses, from now on a number of considerably heavier tractor units and lorries, such as the eight-

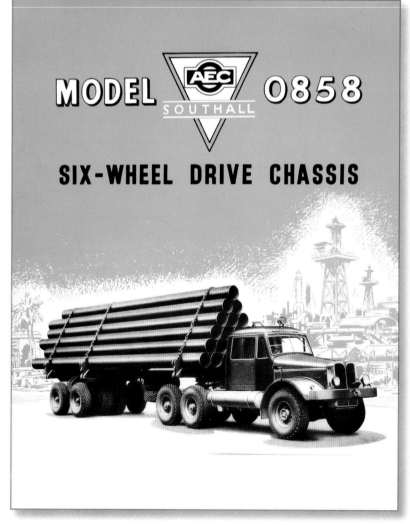

The 0858 was designed for heavy duty work, both on and off road. Its motor was AEC's own 9.6-litre six-cylinder diesel and transmission was by way of a four-speed main gearbox coupled to an auxiliary 'box which had low, direct and high ratios as well provision for six- or four- (rear) wheel drive.

wheeled Mammoth Major of 1934, began to leave the Southall factory. In addition to the volume-produced trucks, these were made throughout the years remaining before Great Britain was once again at war with Germany.

During the war years AEC turned its workforce over to making all manner of ordnance as well as armoured fighting vehicles and the immortal Matador four wheel drive gun tractor. With the war over, the company entered into an agreement with Leyland motors whereby, instead of competing for the trolleybus market, the two firms would join forces and build them under the name of British United Traction. Shortly after this, during the last years of the 1940s, AEC bought two other old established commercial vehicle manufacturers, Maudslay and Crossley. Henceforth the group would be known as ACV (Associated Commercial

Vehicles) and within a short while the other two marques became badge-engineered AECs.

Throughout the 1950s, improved and updated versions of the company's various lorries – all bearing names beginning with the letter M, as they had had since the early 1930s – were introduced. Around 1957, to take advantage of the burgeoning construction and development industries both at home and abroad, AEC began to manufacture large, and later very large, dump trucks.

In 1961 AEC gobbled up another rival in the form of Thornycroft, and in 1962 a full merger with Leyland Motors took place. Leyland Motors then merged with BMC (British Motor Corporation) in 1968, and although AEC carried on making trucks and passenger vehicles at Southall the writing was on the wall. By 1979 it was all over and AEC was no more.

Designed specially for overseas markets, the 2481 was badged AEC worldwide apart from South America and Spain, where the company's products where marketed under the name ACLO. It had a 12ft 1in wheelbase and could easily cope with a 16-ton load, which meant an all-up weight of 25 tons. In common with the 0858, it had air brakes supplied by a gearbox-driven compressor.

The 2481 had the 9.6-litre diesel and a four-speed main gearbox. A constant-mesh auxiliary 'box, operated by a separate lever, with ratios of 1.58:1 reduction and a direct drive of 1:1, provided, in conjunction with the main gearbox, five forward speeds. With the low auxiliary gear engaged the main gearbox ratios were increased and the fifth speed was obtained by selecting direct drive in the auxiliary 'box.

TOWER WAGONS

AEC
SOUTHALL
TRADE MARK

AEC's 1948 elevating platform lorry was manufactured by Eagle on a Monarch Mk III truck chassis. It could be raised by means of a hydraulic ram to over 23ft and rotated through 360 degrees by a circular rack and pinion. Monarchs had the 95bhp 7.7-litre AEC diesel.

The simplified instrument panel

By the mid 1950s the heavy range consisted of the four-wheel Mandator and six- or eight-wheeled Mammoth Major. The cabs were becoming dated although the brochures eulogised the 'well spaced and amply proportioned controls' as well as 'the wide angle of vision given by the windscreen and side windows'.

GRADIENT PERFORMANCE

MAXIMUM CALCULATED GRADIENTS WHICH CAN BE CLIMBED USING 9·6 LITRE ENGINE, 7:1 REAR AXLE RATIO AND 10·00—20 TYRES

Gear	Mandator 12 tons gross	Bonneted Mandator 14 tons gross	Mammoth Major 8 22 tons gross	Mammoth Major 6 19 tons gross	Bonneted Mammoth Major 6 21 tons gross
1st	1 in 2·85	1 in 3·35	1 in 5·4	1 in 4·7	1 in 5·2
2nd	1 in 4·4	1 in 5·3	1 in 8·9	1 in 8·5	1 in 8·5
3rd	1 in 7·75	1 in 9·3	1 in 16	1 in 15·4	1 in 15·4
4th	1 in 14·5	1 in 17·7	1 in 35	1 in 32·5	1 in 32·5
Top	1 in 26	1 in 33	1 in 83	1 in 74	1 in 74

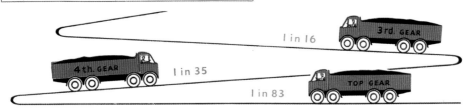

A somewhat strange attempt at modernistic bespoke cab styling on this Mammoth Major six-wheel flat platform lorry on the 16ft 9½in wheelbase. It was also available as a tractor with 11ft 8½in wheelbase, a tipper with one of 14ft 6½in or a longer truck of 18ft 9½in. All lengths also applied to the bonneted version with the exception of the shortest.

Operating for the Bambas Company, of Santa Fe, Argentina, this "Mandator" tractor, with a large capacity refrigerator trailer unit, is used for the transport of perishable foodstuffs.

The Mandator tractor had a wheelbase of 12ft 1in and there was also a tipper with one of 14ft 7in and a truck with 16ft 7in.

An A.E.C. "Mandator" tractor chassis with heavy duty semi-trailer used by the County of Devon Repair Depot for the haulage of road-making equipment.

An all-steel tipping body is fitted to this A.E.C. "Mammoth Major" 8-wheeler which tows an independent tipping trailer. Working at a large hydro-electric scheme in Scotland, the vehicle is one of several operated by the Mitchell Construction Co., Peterborough.

An 8-wheel "Mammoth Major", 4,000 gallon fuel tanker, one of a large number of A.E.C's in the distribution fleet of Shell-Mex and B.P. Ltd.

The twin-steer eight-wheel Mammoth Major shared the same wheelbase dimensions as the six-wheeler with the exception of the shorter as there was no eight-wheeled tractor.

AECs enjoyed almost limitless interchangeability of components, which meant that your vehicle could have either their 9.6-litre or 11.3-litre diesel engine, a five- or six-speed gearbox and, in the case of the Mammoths, various types of rear bogie – a four-spring balance beam type with either single- or twin-axle drive, a fully articulated unit with twin-axle drive with double-reduction bevel, or one with overhead worm with third differential in the forward axle.

A high-sided tipping body is fitted to this A.E.C. "Mammoth Major" 8-wheeler, operated by the Queensland Cement & Lime Co. Ltd., Australia.

This "Mammoth Major" 8 special bulk grain end-tipper is operated by William Simmons Ltd., Leighton Buzzard. It has fixed high sides and rear double doors.

The Mustang had been around for a while, firstly as a Maudslay, and 1958 saw the introduction of the Mk II version. Wheelbase was 19ft and it had the 7.7-litre AEC AV470 six-cylinder engine with a five-speed gearbox. Air pressure assistance for the hydraulic brakes was supplied by an engine-driven compressor.

Although the sales material spoke of progressive design, just exactly who the copywriters imagined might think that flexible engine mountings and by-pass thermostats were something to boast about in the late 1950s defeats me, and a light-alloy sump was hardly a technological breakthrough.

A SIX-WHEELER WITH EVENLY DISTRIBUTED AXLE LOADINGS

Mustang Twin Steer
Mark II
18 TONS GROSS CHASSIS

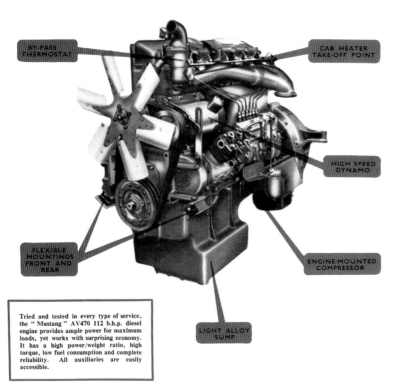

BY-PASS THERMOSTAT

CAB HEATER TAKE-OFF POINT

HIGH SPEED DYNAMO

FLEXIBLE MOUNTINGS FRONT AND REAR

ENGINE-MOUNTED COMPRESSOR

LIGHT ALLOY SUMP

Tried and tested in every type of service, the " Mustang " AV470 112 b.h.p. diesel engine provides ample power for maximum loads, yet works with surprising economy. It has a high power/weight ratio, high torque, low fuel consumption and complete reliability. All auxiliaries are easily accessible.

The "Mustang" frame has all the strength needed for a 12-ton payload, yet by sound design its weight has been brought down to achieve a kerb chassis weight of 4 tons 18½ cwts.

Mercury Tractor
471/505

The 1964 Mercury Tractor epitomised the look of the firm's current range. Although the vehicles appeared much more modern and were advertised more slickly, a good deal of the engineering had had little radical change from the previous decade.

The Mercury Tractor's 8ft wheelbase was a popular one amongst several manufacturers of tractor units. There were two engine options: an updated version of the old 112 x 130mm AEC 7.7-litre diesel, the AV471, which had been persuaded to turn over at 2400rpm to give 143bhp, and the AV505, which was the same engine with its bore increased to 116mm, producing an extra 11bhp at the same revs.

POWER BRAKING

Direct air pressure brakes with anti-fade brake linings working in heavily ribbed drums give smooth and powerful braking under varying load and road conditions. Brake drum diameter, 15½ in. Linings, 5 in. wide front, and 7 in. wide rear. Total friction area: footbrake, 712 sq. in., handbrake, 416 sq. in. An exhaust brake and separate front and rear brake circuits can be fitted.

SHOCK-FREE CLUTCH

The tough single-plate hydraulically operated clutch combines ease of operation with the ability to absorb transmission shocks. Smooth take-up and a non-slip drive through a friction plate area of 237 sq. in.

AIR-ASSISTED HANDBRAKE

An air valve controlled by free movement in the hand lever pivot admits air from a separate compartment in the reservoir, to the triple diaphragm rear brake chambers. For parking the brake is held by a normal ratchet, the air pressure being automatically released.

HIGH EFFICIENCY ENGINE

SIX-SPEED OVERDRIVE GEARBOX

Smooth, sure, foolproof gearshifting through six ratios including overdrive. Precision finished gears promote long life of this robust unit, which is both compact and uncomplicated. Ratios, 1st, 6·63:1; 2nd, 4·44:1; 3rd, 2·54:1; 4th, 1·53:1; 5th, 1:1; 6th (overdrive), 0·75:1; reverse, 6·59:1. Provision is made for fitting a normal duty power take-off and, with a casing modification, a full torque unit.

'Saloon car comfort and styling' read the brochure describing the steel tilt cab. I cannot bring to mind exactly which saloon car but I do know what they were trying to say.

The motorway age was dawning and the Mercury, with its top speed of over 60mph, awaits its driver, but this idyllic concept of 40 years ago is a stark contrast to the reality of the early 21st century.

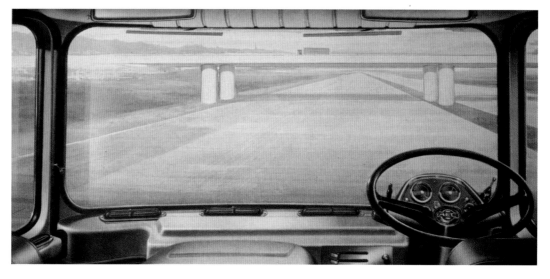

ALBION

Two former employees of the Scottish firm Arrol-Johnston set up on their own account in 1900 to produce vehicles in very much the same vein as they had in their previous employment. Curiously named dog carts, these vehicles usually had under-floor engines, solid rubber tyres and, at first, tiller steering. By their very name it was evident that they were little more than motorised versions of horse-drawn conveyances. In 1903 they embarked on some mild modernisation and, although largely failing to embrace the advantages of the pneumatic tyre, started to build cars designed for carrying shooting and hunting parties on the Scottish estates, along with a commercial derivative, all having a fairly puny twin-cylinder engine rated at 16hp.

1910 heralded a much larger four-cylinder petrol-engined truck with chain drive which was destined to remain in production until the mid-1920s, over 5000 of them being supplied to the armed forces during Wold War 1 in 3-ton form.

Cars had ceased to be made by the firm before the war, but charabancs and single-deck buses were now produced alongside the commercials, and various versions of the range were introduced during the 1920s, from 1_ tons up to medium weight.

The company was restructured during 1930, its name changing from Albion Motor Car Company to simply Albion Motors, and during the following year a fresh 2-tonner was announced.

For 1935 Albion brought out a new 5½-tonner along with a 13-ton six-wheeler, and shortly afterwards acquired the remnants, including the factory premises, of the other long-established Scottish commercial vehicle firm, Halley, which had to throw in the towel after failing to weather the setbacks of the late 1920s. Albion by now was also working on the development of its own diesel engine. This was to give the company the option of independence from the almost universal use of Gardner engines by commercial vehicle manufacturers during the 1930s, and Albion's new diesel engines went into the six- and eight-wheelers immediately prior to the war.

During the next five years the workforce found

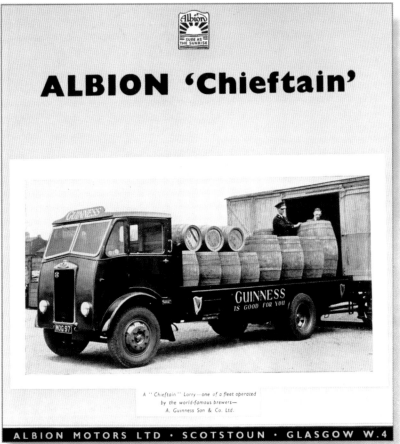

ALBION 'Chieftain'

A "Chieftain" Lorry—one of a fleet operated by the world-famous brewers—A. Guinness Son & Co. Ltd.

ALBION MOTORS LTD · SCOTSTOUN · GLASGOW W.4

The standard van was built on the two longer chassis.

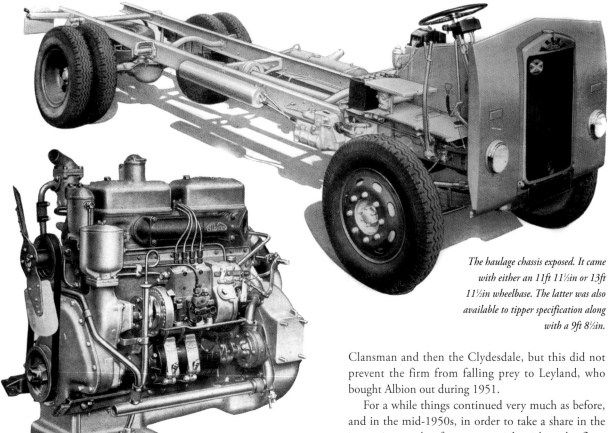

The haulage chassis exposed. It came with either an 11ft 11½in or 13ft 11½in wheelbase. The latter was also available to tipper specification along with a 9ft 8½in.

The 4.88-litre diesel engine was Albion's own EN286, which produced 75bhp at 2000rpm. Albion also made the five-speed gearbox.

themselves flat out producing four wheel drive 3-ton trucks, artillery tractors, 10-ton 4x6s and various other specialised vehicles.

A patriotic start was made after the war with the Chieftain, which was joined within a short while by the Clansman and then the Clydesdale, but this did not prevent the firm from falling prey to Leyland, who bought Albion out during 1951.

For a while things continued very much as before, and in the mid-1950s, in order to take a share in the increasing market for commercials with under-floor engines, the Claymore was introduced. From then on, however, Leyland influence was increasingly evident in the Scottish product, both visually and under the skin, which resulted in the Scottish version of the late 1950s Leyland Octopus emerging as the Caledonian. The official end for Albion came in 1972, and from then on, Scottish connotation notwithstanding, Leyland's north-of-the-border products became known for what they were

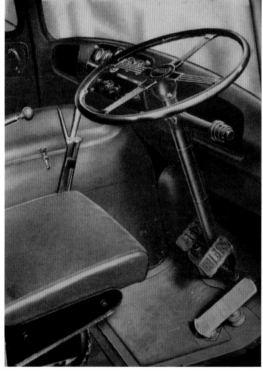

Above and above right: By now Leyland owned Albion, so the new Chieftain's cab was common with that firm's Comet.

There were Three haulage chassis of 10ft 3in, 12ft and 13ft 6in wheelbase, plus a tipper of 8ft 6in. An Albion four-cylinder diesel was still used but this was the EN335 of 5.5 litres. The gearbox had five-speeds as standard but an another speed was available at extra cost.

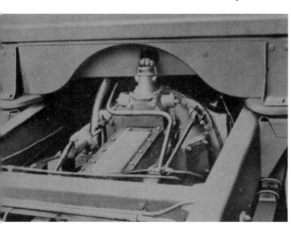

Rubber-mounted cab.

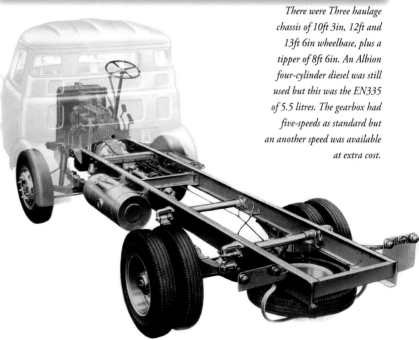

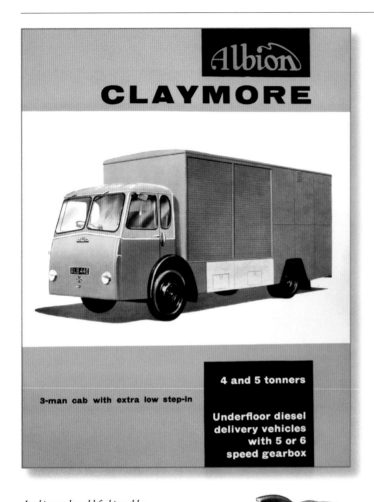

Albion
CLAYMORE

3-man cab with extra low step-in

4 and 5 tonners

Underfloor diesel delivery vehicles with 5 or 6 speed gearbox

Pressed-steel Chieftain Series II cab.

Looking rather old-fashioned by 1963 when this brochure was printed, the Claymore had first appeared in the mid-1950s.

Epicyclic hub reduction gear.

The 'roomy 3 man cab' might be better described with that lovely estate agent's term 'deceptively spacious'. Nor was it 'up to the minute' by this time, though the under-floor engine did give a clear floor space.

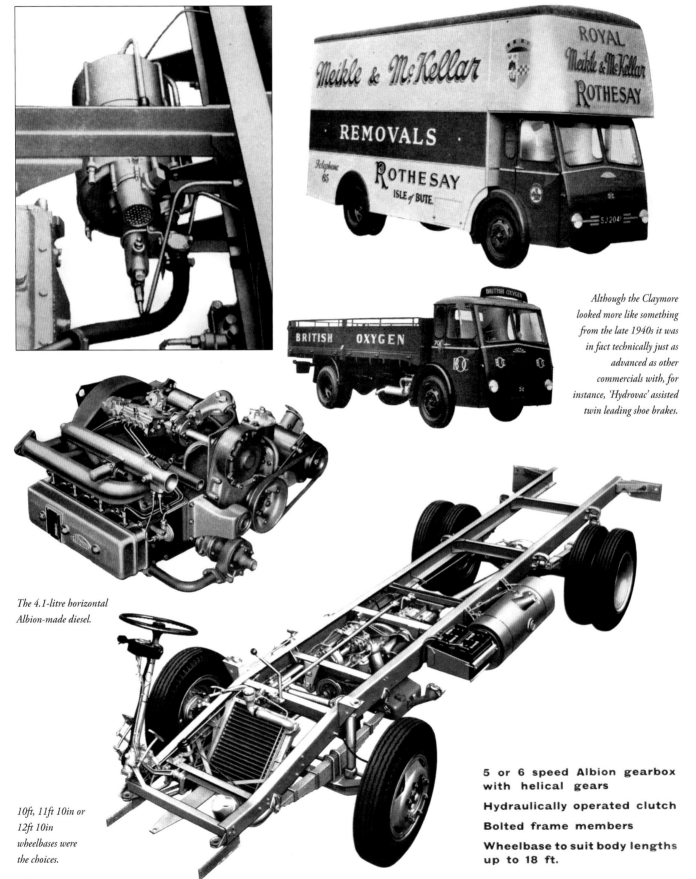

Although the Claymore looked more like something from the late 1940s it was in fact technically just as advanced as other commercials with, for instance, 'Hydrovac' assisted twin leading shoe brakes.

The 4.1-litre horizontal Albion-made diesel.

10ft, 11ft 10in or 12ft 10in wheelbases were the choices.

5 or 6 speed Albion gearbox with helical gears

Hydraulically operated clutch

Bolted frame members

Wheelbase to suit body lengths up to 18 ft.

ATKINSON

Originally a sales outlet for Sentinel steam lorries, which were made in Scotland, Atkinson and Company in Lancashire seemingly had the carpet pulled from under their feet when Sentinel decided to move down to England as well as henceforth taking care of its own marketing. In spite of the country being immersed in the war in Europe, Atkinson decided in 1916 to set up as a manufacturer of steam lorries, adopting what appeared to be the most desirable features of the Sentinel and other makes. This brave move paid off, and by the early years of the 1920s Atkinson was well established, with a choice of either rigid or articulated steam lorries on offer, but this success was short-lived. The remainder of the decade saw the firm lurching from one ill-starred attempt to resurrect itself to the next. Such efforts included branching out into the manufacture of small railway locomotives and the acquisition of Leyland's remaining steam lorry stock. Leyland must have been more than happy to relieve a competitor of some money for what it saw as an encumbrance.

By 1930, in order to stay afloat, Atkinson had returned to its roots by reverting to being merely a commercial vehicle repair depot, but this move was of no avail and the receiver was called in. No doubt at a bargain price, a small consortium of local business people bought the firm to keep the doors open. Within a couple of years new designs had been drawn up and their construction was under way.

Henceforth the firm was to be known as Atkinson Lorries (1933) Ltd, and a comprehensive range from 7 up to 15 tons became available through the remaining years before the war. In fact availability was more or less in name only as the company's tiny manufacturing capability would not have allowed large orders to be fulfilled, and in reality only a few dozen new Atkinsons took to the roads of the later 1930s. The war brought a windfall in form of contracts to build several hundred of their six- and eight-wheelers and Atkinson expanded accordingly to fulfil these, coping with the shortage of Gardner engines, which they had utilised pre-war, by fitting AEC units in the same way as other firms.

The 644 was the baby of the Atkinson range in 1947. Wheelbase was 12ft 8in and the engine was a 3.8-litre Gardner which pushed out 53bhp at 2000rpm. The five-speed gearbox was the company's own; pre-war it had used David Brown 'boxes but difficulties encountered in their supply had encouraged Atkinson to produce one themselves.

This 4-WHEELED 6-TONNER is a real WORKER

Model L.644—4-wheeled 6-tonner is another of the ATKINSON range of Vehicles. With an unladen weight of under 3 tons, and fitted with a Gardner 4.LK type Diesel Engine, it is designed to run at a legal speed of 30 m.p.h.

Every detail of design and construction has been meticulously studied to ensure a vehicle of the highest attainable performance in its class, coupled with economical operation and long life.

We confidently present the L.644 as a vehicle which will further enhance ATKINSON prestige.

MODEL L 644

Atkinson

FINEST LORRIES ON THE ROADS OF BRITAIN

Knight of the road

The old range was revived for the early peacetime years, and the first radical departure from this was in 1952 when the company began to branch out into the manufacture of public transport vehicles which resulted, two years later, in a name change to Atkinson Vehicles Ltd.

In addition to buses and their regular lorries, in the mid-1950s Atkinson began to make very large capacity tractor units as well as dump trucks and snow-clearing vehicles under government contracts.

Following the general trend, by 1960 the road haulage range had had fibreglass cabs and wrap-around divided windscreens for a couple of years, although the traditional radiator was retained. A little later came an offer from Pickfords heavy transport department to undertake the joint development of a wider range of tractor units, with Pickfords obviously having first call on the resulting production.

All in all the firm was in a pretty healthy state, and for the rest of the 1960s continued to enhance its range to take in the industry's every need, from heavy site work to oversize road haulage. Success made it a prime target for takeover bids, of which there were more than one, with Seddon winning the day as the 1970s dawned. It was not to be too long before Seddon itself was taken over by International Harvester, who oversaw the birth of a new generation of vehicles which from now on was to carry the name Seddon-Atkinson.

For the 1948 brochure cover Atkinson launched into almost Arthurian fantasy courtesy of artist Stanley Chew. By one of life's amazing coincidences I went to school with his sons and came to know their father later when he had gone on to be one of England's foremost painters of pub signs.

The 745 in truck form, as well as being able to carry 7½ tons, would happily pull an 8-ton trailer. It came with either a 15ft or 13ft 6in wheelbase. The 745 was also made as a tipper with 10ft 9in wheelbase or as a tractor of 8ft 9in. Like all other Atkinsons it was powered by Gardner, in this case the 85bhp five-cylinder 5LW.

21

This is the 1266 12-ton 15ft 1½in wheelbase truck, also made as a tipper with 13ft 3in wheelbase. The truck version was made with either double-drive rear bogie or single-axle drive. Power unit was a 102bhp Gardner 6LW.

Atkinson
12·ton 6·wheeler

HOMEPRIDE

Model 1266

with GARDNER 6LW Engine

This 12-ton 6-wheeler has a 6-cylinder engine and 5-speed gear box, and is an acknowledged leader in its class.

Behind it is the ATKINSON tradition which places quality and performance first.

The 1266 played a notable part during the war years. The experience thus gained enabled us to produce a post-war 1266 whose reliability and performance is truly outstanding.

If and when a better 6-wheeler can be built, it will emerge from the ATKINSON organisation.

John Bull, clasping his own miniature Atkinson, looks down from the heavens upon the 15-ton L1586 eight-wheeler. This had a 17ft 8¼in wheelbase but it was also made as a tipper of 15ft 1½in. Both were fitted with the Gardner 6LW and, like all the firm's trucks, had an in-house five-speed gearbox.

Typically
BRITISH

More fantasy, with the export M1266 six-wheeler bound for Port Elizabeth, South Africa. In addition to its 12-ton capacity it could handle a 6-ton trailer.

An export heavyweight.

Sorry, another L644, although this one is from 1949. I just couldn't resist it. One could be excused for thinking that Atkinson had branched out into jousting tournaments as a sideline.

Knight of the road

MODEL L644 4 WHEELED 6 TONNER

Model L.644: four-wheeled, six-tonner, is another of the ATKINSON range of Vehicles. With an unladen weight of under three tons, and fitted with a Gardner 4 LK type Diesel Engine, it is designed to run at a legal speed of 30 m.p.h. Every detail of design and construction has been meticulously studied to ensure a vehicle of the highest attainable performance in its class, coupled with economical operation and long life. We confidently present the L.644 as a vehicle which will further enhance ATKINSON prestige.

Atkinson
LEADS THE WAY

Model S 744
7½-ton Tipper

The S744 tipper with 10ft 9in wheelbase and Gardner 4LW engine.

An L1586 tanker with 3000-gallon capacity.

THE KNIGHT OFF THE ROAD

THE **OMEGA** 6X6 CROSS-COUNTRY VEHICLE

A.P.L. 101—Oct. 1959

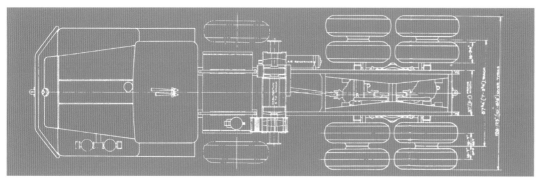
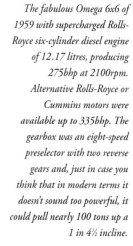

The fabulous Omega 6x6 of 1959 with supercharged Rolls-Royce six-cylinder diesel engine of 12.17 litres, producing 275bhp at 2100rpm. Alternative Rolls-Royce or Cummins motors were available up to 335bhp. The gearbox was an eight-speed preselector with two reverse gears and, just in case you think that in modern terms it doesn't sound too powerful, it could pull nearly 100 tons up a 1 in 4½ incline.

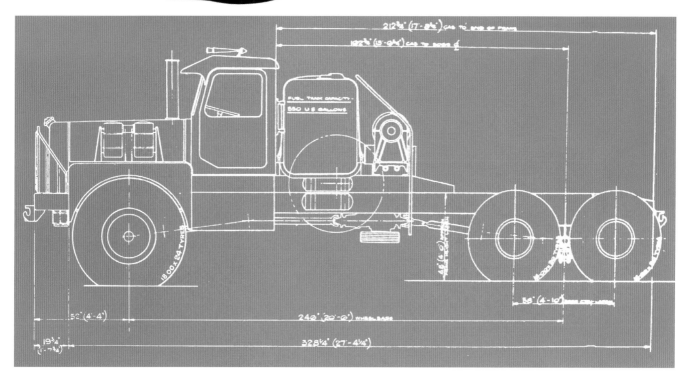

HOME RANGE

The method of cab construction was to your choice: lightweight coachbuilt, standard coachbuilt, de-luxe heavy duty coachbuilt with fibreglass panels, steel frame de-luxe heavy duty with fibreglass panels, or all steel. As on most other commercial vehicles a heater was still an extra, and although flashing direction indicators were on the way they were still optional.

TYPE	GROSS WGHT. TONS	GROSS WGHT. LBS.	BODY SIZE	PAY-LOAD TONS	WHEEL-BASE
MODEL					
TRACTOR GROUP					
T 744	16	35840	FOR ARTIC SEMI TRAIL"	12	8'-9"
T 745	22	49280	,,	18	,,
T 746	28	62720	,,	24	,,
T 746X	28	,,	,,	,,	,,
ST 1044LW	16	35840	SCAMMELL ARTIC.TRAIL	12	,,
ST 1045	,,	,,	,,	,,	,,
TIPPER GROUP					
S 644 LW	11	24640	5/6 CUBIC YARDS	6	10'-8"
S 744	12	26880	6/7 ,,	7	10'-9"
S 745	,,	,,	,, ,,	,,	,,
S 746	,,	,,	,, ,,	,,	,,
M 745	,,	,,	,, ,,	,,	12'-4"
M 746	,,	,,	,, ,,	,,	,,
S 945	14	31360	,, ,,	9	10'-9"
S 946	,,	,,	,, ,,	,,	,,
S 946X	,,	,,	,, ,,	,,	,,
FREIGHT GROUP					
L 644	9	19160	16'-0"x7'-6	6	12'-4 3/4"
L 644LW	11	24640	17'-6"x7'-6	,,	13'-5 1/4"
L 644 LWL	,,	,,	20'-0"x7'-6	,,	16'-0 1/2"
L 645 LW	14	31360	17'-6"x7'-6	10	13'-5 1/4"
L 645 LWL	,,	,,	20'-0"x7'-6	,,	16'-0 1/2"
L 744	12	26880	17'-6"x8'-0	7	13'-6"
L 745	,,	,,	,,	,,	,,
L 746 L	,,	,,	20'-0"x8'-0	,,	16'-0 1/2"
L 746XL	,,	,,	,,	,,	,,
L 945	14	31360	17'-6"x8'-0	9	13'-6"
L 946	,,	,,	,,	,,	,,
L 946X	,,	,,	,,	,,	,,
L 945L	,,	,,	20'-0"x8'-0	,,	16'-0 1/2"
L 946L	,,	,,	,,	,,	,,
L 946XL	,,	,,	,,	,,	,,

THE ENGINES LISTED BELOW CAN BE SUPPLIED AS ALTERNATIVES TO THE STANDARD ENGINE ON MOST MODELS

TYPE	BORE INS.	STROKE INS.	MAX. B.H.P. AT R.P.M.	MAX. TORQUE AT R.P.M.	CAPACITY LITRES	USE WITH GEARBOX TYPE
GARDNER 4 LW	4 1/4	6	75 @ 1700	237 @ 1300	5·6	045
GARDNER 5 LW	,,	,,	94 @ 1700	300 @ 1300	7·0	5450, 557
GARDNER 6 LW	,,	,,	112 @ 1700	358 @ 1300	8·4	557, AK or 56-55
GARDNER 6 LX	4 3/4	,,	150 @ 1700	485 @ 1100	10·45	557/480, AK6-55
CUMMINS HU6	4 7/8	,,	158 @ 1800	490 @ 1250	11·0	AK6-75
CUMMINS NH6	5 1/8	,,	212 @ 2100	580 @ 1600	12·2	,,
ROLLS ROYCE C6N	,,	,,	178 @ 1800	547 @ 1300	12·17	561

TYPE	NO. OF WHLS	GROSS WGHT. LBS.	GROSS WGHT. KGS.	BODY SIZE	WHEEL BASE
HEAVY DUTY TRACTOR RANGE					
OMEGA I	6	200000	90718	FOR ARTIC. SEMI TRAIL.	20'-6"
OMEGA III	"	"	"	"	"
STANDARD TRACTOR RANGE					
T.746 A.	4	62720	28449	FOR ARTIC. SEMI TRAIL.	8'-9"
T.746 X A.	"	"	"	"	"
T.746 C A.	"	"	"	"	10'-9"
T.1366 X A.	6	78400	35562	"	10'-11"
T.1366 C A.	"	"	"	"	13'-3"
MEDIUM TRACTOR RANGE					
B T.1366 X A.	6	112000	50802	FOR ARTIC. SEMI TRAIL.	14'-0"
B T.1366 C A.	"	"	"	"	"
B T.1366 C L A.	"	"	"	"	17'-0"
TIPPER RANGE					
S.946 A.	4	31360	14224	6/7 CUBIC YARDS	10'-9"
S.946 X A.	"	"	"	"	"
S.1366 A.	6	44800	20321	10/11 "	13'-3"
S.1786 X A.	8	53760	24385	12/13 "	15'-1¾"
S.1786 X L A.	"	"	"	"	16'-7½"
S.2086 C A.	"	67200	28449	15/16 "	15'-1¾"
DUMPER RANGE					
DT.745 A.	4	31360	14224	6/7 CUBIC YARDS	8'-9"
DT.746 A.	"	"	"	"	"
DT.746 X A.	"	"	"	"	"
DT.746 C A.	"	"	"	"	"
DT.1366 X A.	6	58240	26417	9/10 "	11'-3"
DT.1366 C A.	"	"	"	"	"
DT.1366 R R A.	"	"	"	"	"

On export models the choice of engines was virtually the same as on home models, as were the cabs, but extras for export included a tropical radiator, left-hand drive and other options suitable for the destination country. If it had been Iraq, for example, the vehicle would have been consigned to the distributor Abdul Razak Freih, Rashid Street, Baghdad.

EXPORT RANGE

Three- or four-man cab Prime Mover with either a Rolls-Royce or Cummins engine of 250bhp.

The superb 1962 brochure cover. Within, it commences: 'We have endeavoured to illustrate in this brochure a typical selection from the range of models emanating from the Atkinson factory."

ATKINSON VEHICLES LTD. WINERY LANE WALTON-LE-DALE NR. PRESTON ENGLAND

This brewery four-wheeler has a 94bhp Gardner 5LW and a five-speed gearbox.

Eight-wheelers such as this normally had a 150bhp 10.45-litre Gardner LX motor and either five- or six-speed transmission with auxiliary step-up or step-down gearbox.

An articulated tanker based on a four-wheel extended-wheelbase tractor powered by a Gardner 6LW in conjunction with a six-speed gearbox; equipped with an all-steel cab for use in Australia.

This six-wheeler tipper has a special body with front mounted rams. The cab is fibreglass and the engine is an 8.4-litre Gardner 6LW.

AUSTIN

During the First World War the Austin Motor Company, founded in 1906 by Herbert Austin after he had resigned as manager of Wolseley Motors, was contracted to supply around 2000 of a rather quirky lorry which it had designed. Its unusual features included a mid-mounted differential from which radiated a pair of propeller shafts, one for each wheel, arranged thus in order to keep the load area as low as possible. In use the vehicle was beset with problems but Austin persevered with it and other similar models until the early 1920s. Thereafter the sole commercial produced of over 1-ton was a derivative of the Austin four-cylinder 20hp car.

From then on the company offered small commercials based on its range of cars, with even the tiny Austin Seven available in van and Milk Delivery versions. It was the late 1930s before any strictly commercial chassis were to leave the factory, at

For firms such as Austin it was relatively simple to resume civilian production after the war had ended.

which time Austin re-entered the field with a selection of lorries up to 3-ton payload. The events of 1939 accelerated this process and during the next six years the company produced well over 100,000 four- and six-wheeled trucks, as well as towing vehicles based on the smallest of their recently introduced commercial range.

Within a year of the end of the war in Europe Austin unveiled something completely fresh in the form of their 25cwt Three Way Loader, which in many ways pre-empted the various multi-stop delivery vans that were to become fashionable more than a decade later. Happy to leave the heavy haulage business to others the company shortly afterwards announced a 5-ton truck which was then joined by the Loadstar series of 2-, 3- and 5-tonners in 1950.

During 1952 Austin merged with Morris to form the British Motor Corporation and from then on

AUSTIN

2-TON & 5-TON
COMMERCIAL
VEHICLES

Throughout the world, "Austin" is synonymous with dependability, and dependability, where commercial transport is concerned, is of paramount importance.

These vehicles will meet all demands made upon them; ample power with safe and easy handling gives confidence to the driver and satisfactory return to the operator.

AUSTIN DEPENDABILITY IS NEEDED FOR THE TASKS OF RECONSTRUCTION

AUS 46

PRICES
As and from MAY 12th, 1941,
IN GREY PRIMING AT WORKS

2-TON LONG WHEELBASE
Chassis £375
Chassis and Cab £415
Platform Lorry £455
Dropside Lorry £460

5-TON LONG WHEELBASE
Chassis £465
Chassis and Cab £505
Platform Lorry £560
Dropside Lorry £570

5-TON SHORT WHEELBASE
Chassis £450
Chassis and Cab £490
Hydraulic Tipper £590

Prices are subject to alteration without notice.
THE AUSTIN MOTOR COMPANY, LIMITED.
For Pub. No. 2167.

what was considered the best from both companies was distilled into the BMC range. Broadly speaking this meant that forward-control vehicles owed more to Morris influence whereas those with normal control were born of Austin thinking - sometimes, confusingly, the same vehicle was marketed as either an Austin or a BMC.

For 1957 a completely fresh design appeared in the form of the 701 7-tonner and then, two years later, the corporation brought out the rather ugly FG delivery vehicles ranging from 2 to 4 tons which, in spite of their looks, were destined to remain current for the next 20 years.

A move was made to a purpose-built factory in West Lothian, Scotland, during 1961 where, from then on, all commercials other than lightweight models were to be produced. A new forward-control model was introduced, while the ageing 7-tonner was modernised and then finally, in 1965, given a five-speed gearbox, air brakes and a tilting cab.

In 1968, during the second Labour government formed by Harold Wilson, and at his behest, the British Motor Corporation joined forces with the Leyland Motor Corporation, the result of which was the ill starred British Leyland Motor Corporation.

From then on the smaller commercials were badged as Austin-Morris whilst the rest became Leylands. For rather more than 15 years the whole unwieldy conglomeration of car and lorry companies meandered through a catalogue of disasters which, as far as the commercials were concerned, started on a different path when DAF of Holland took them on in 1986. DAF itself went bankrupt during 1993 but the truck side of things managed to get going again, while the light commercial business was bought by the management and became LDV. By 1998 DAF, Leyland, call it what you will, had been added to the US giant PACCAR's list of possessions and the vehicles continue to be manufactured and marketed with at least a semblance of separate identities.

The engine was the well-proven Austin six-cylinder ohv of 3459cc, for which they claimed 67.5bhp at 2900rpm. This was mated to a conventional four-speed gearbox.

The 5-ton tipper had a power takeoff point on the gearbox which would accommodate any standard type of power tipping gear.

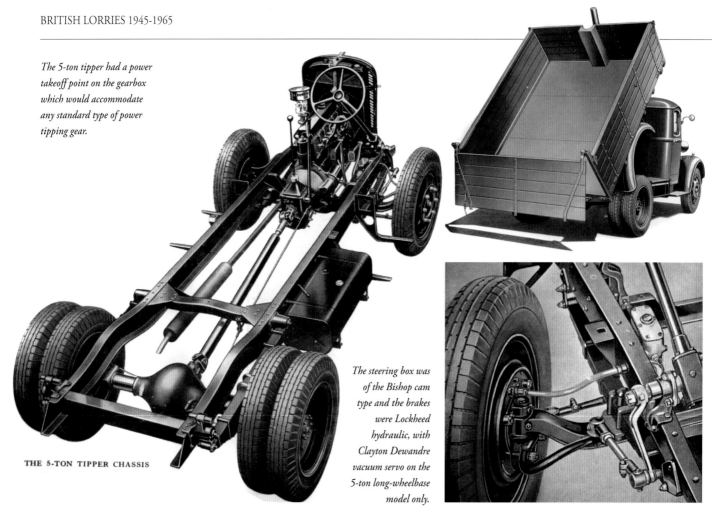

THE 5-TON TIPPER CHASSIS

The steering box was of the Bishop cam type and the brakes were Lockheed hydraulic, with Clayton Dewandre vacuum servo on the 5-ton long-wheelbase model only.

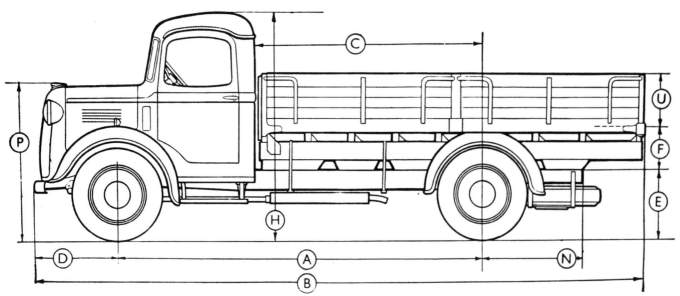

VEHICLE	A	B	C	D	*E	F	*H	J	L	M	N	*P	S	T	U
2-TON LONG WHEELBASE LORRY	11'2"	18'9"	6'11½"	2'6¼"	2'1⅛"	1'3⅞"	6'7½"	6'4¼"	6'8"	3'1"	3'1"	4'6"	6'2"	11'6"	18"
5-TON LONG WHEELBASE LORRY	13'1¾"	21'3"	8'11¼"	2'6¼"	2'3⅛"	1'5¼"	6'9¾"	6'4¼"	6'11"	3'1"	3'5¼"	4'8¼"	6'7"	14'0"	18"
5-TON SHORT WHEELBASE END TIPPER	9'3¾"	15'6"	5'1¼"	2'6¼"	2'3⅛"	1'3⅞"	6'9¾"	6'4¼"	7'0"	3'1"	2'9"	4'8¼"	6'7"	8'3"	2'3½"

* VEHICLE LADEN

The 300 cubic feet body was constructed from steel panels on a wood frame and had steel wearing plates for the wood floor and sides to waist height.

The engine was the four-cylinder ohv 2199cc A70 petrol unit and, in the case of a major overhaul, could easily be withdrawn from the front along with gearbox and radiator.

At the rear and on both sides double doors on surface-fitting hinges swung right back to give unobstructed access to the interior.

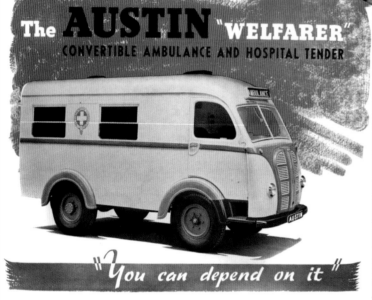

The AUSTIN "WELFARER"
CONVERTIBLE AMBULANCE AND HOSPITAL TENDER

"You can depend on it"

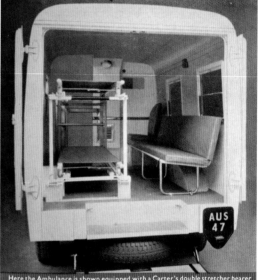

Here the Ambulance is shown equipped with a Carter's double stretcher bearer (left) with a seat for six persons (right). The seat for the attendant is clearly shown at forward end of body (opposite side door). On the right above and between the two windows may be seen the thermostat control for the heater unit.

Interior appointments included a Carter's double stretcher bearer, seating for six persons as well as an attendant at the front, and thermostatically controlled heating. Window glass was semi-opaque to provide privacy for the occupants.

Spare wheel cover hinged downwards to provide a pair of steps.

The illuminated 'Ambulance' sign was provided at no extra charge but, including interior fitments as shown, the price of £871 against £645 for the basic van (both without purchase tax) probably more than allowed for this.

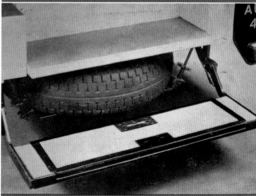

When rear step is lowered, a further step is exposed and the arrangement provides easy access to interior. The recessed handle on lower step is again used to raise step back to closed position. A convenient fixture for the spare wheel is provided beneath step.

AUSTIN Carrimore

SIX · WHEELERS

THE ANSWER TO EVERY TRANSPORT PROBLEM FOR ANY LOADS UP TO 10 TONS

The tractor had Austin's staple six-cylinder ohv petrol engine of just under 4 litres, which served in commercials as well as Princess motor cars.

DETACHABLE AXLES

A perfect loading ramp for heavy and awkward loads is obtained by the use of a CARRIMORE low loading detachable axle Semi-Trailer.

The whole axle assembly with Springs and Mudguards is instantly removed by merely lifting two self-locking plates. No spanners or tools of any kind are required.

for **MAXIMUM CAPACITY**

or **MINIMUM HEIGHT**

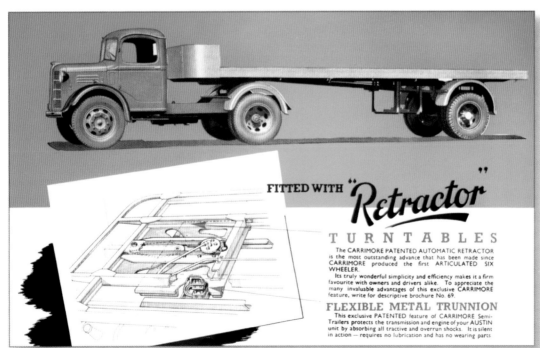

FITTED WITH *"Retractor"*

T U R N T A B L E S

The CARRIMORE PATENTED AUTOMATIC RETRACTOR is the most outstanding advance that has been made since CARRIMORE produced the first ARTICULATED SIX WHEELER.
Its truly wonderful simplicity and efficiency makes it a firm favourite with owners and drivers alike. To appreciate the many invaluable advantages of this exclusive CARRIMORE feature, write for descriptive brochure No. 69.

FLEXIBLE METAL TRUNNION

This exclusive PATENTED feature of CARRIMORE Semi-Trailers protects the transmission and engine of your AUSTIN unit by absorbing all tractive and overrun shocks. It is silent in action — requires no lubrication and has no wearing parts.

This system was an alternative to the Scammell for articulated trailers.

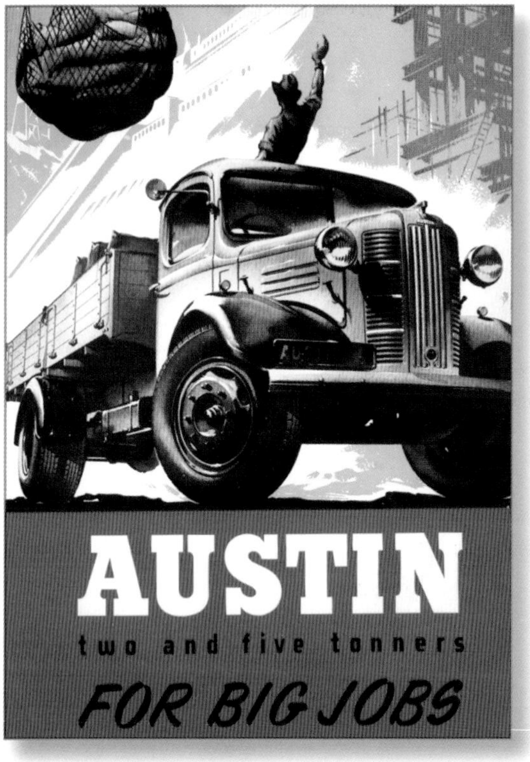

I can well imagine that the cover of this brochure raised a titter amongst school boys who happened upon it during the 1950s.

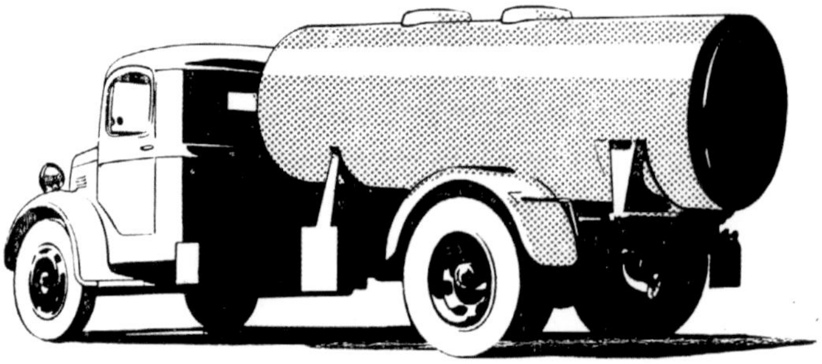

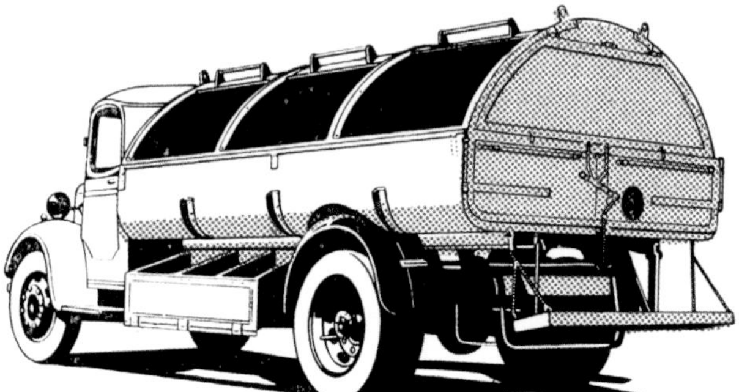

The Austin Loadstar provided the basis for Morris's ugly clone but this is prior to the merger which produced BMC. It was powered by the Princess engine.

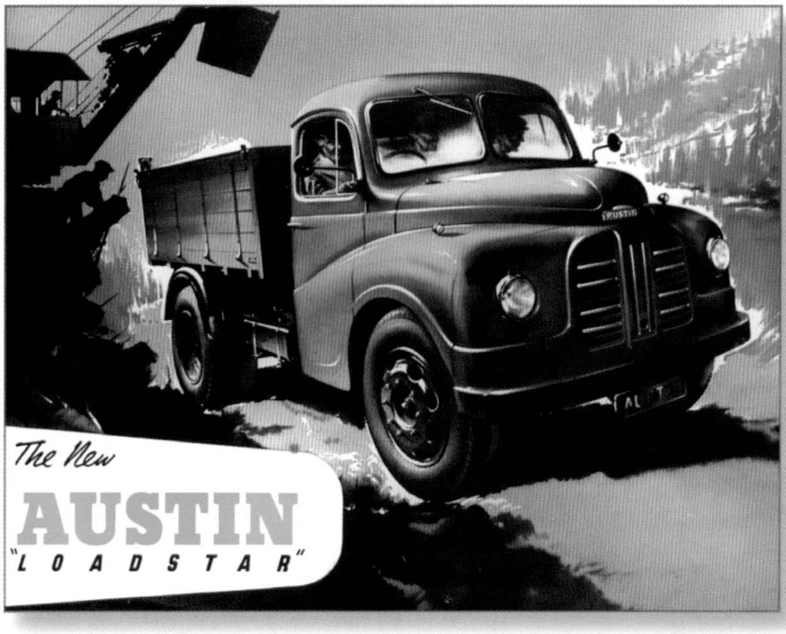

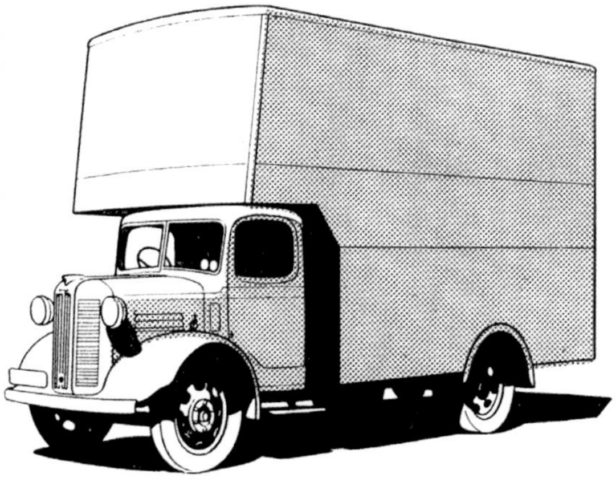

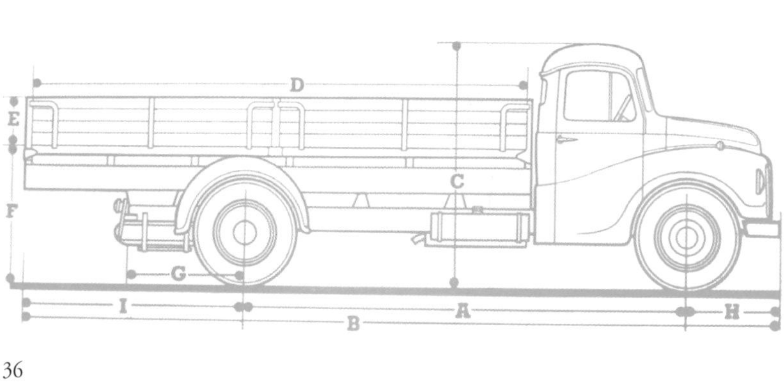

LEADING DIMENSIONS		2-ton L.W.B.			5-ton L.W.B.			5-ton S.W.B. TIPPER		
		English ft.	ins.	Metric m.	English ft.	ins.	Metric m.	English ft.	ins.	Metric m.
Vheelbase ...	A	11	2	3·40	13	1¾	4·01	9	7	2·92
)verall Length	B	19	3	5·87	21	8⅞	6·63	15	11⅛	4·85
Overall Height (unladen) ...	C	6	9⅞	2·07	7	1⅝	2·17	7	1⅛	2·16
Interior Body Length	D	11	6	3·50	14	0	4·27	8	3	2·51
Height of Body Sides	E	1	6	0·46	1	6	0·46	2	3½	0·70
Height of Body Floor (unladen) ...	F	3	8½	1·12	4	0	1·22	3	10	1·17
Centre of Rear Hub to End of Frame	G	3	1	0·94	3	5¼	1·05	2	9	0·84
Centre of Front Hub to Bumper ...	H	2	9	0·84	2	9	0·84	2	9	0·84
Centre of Rear Hub to End of Body	I	5	4	1·63	5	10⅛	1·78	3	7⅛	1·09
Body Interior Width (max.)		6	2	1·88	6	7	2·01	6	7	2·01
Cab Interior Width (max. at waist) ...		5	2	1·57	5	2	1·57	5	2	1·57
Overall Width of Truck		6	7 11/16	2·02	7	3⅝	2·22	7	0	2·13
Track—front		5	5	1·65	5	4	1·63	5	4	1·63
Track—rear		5	3	1·60	5	6 11/16	1·69	5	6 11/16	1·69
Ground Clearance ...			10	0·25		10½	0·26		10½	0·26
Turning Circle... ...		48	0	14·63	55	0	16·76	40	0	12·19

'When sailing dates must be met, perishable goods carried quickly, contractors' materials transported, dependable Austin trucks will be found leading the way', reads the brochure. This is the 5-ton long-wheelbase truck.

'A driver's eye view through the toughened glass windscreen' – but has the driver taken his hands off the wheel, mesmerised at the scene unfolding in front of him?

The 5-ton long-wheelbase chassis. By now Austin was part of BMC and the name Loadstar had been dropped for the series.

The 5-ton short-wheelbase tipper in standard form. A number of alternative tipping gears and body styles, in both wood and metal, could be supplied.

AUSTIN 5-ton tipper

The 5-ton short wheelbase end tipper is a thoroughbred, toughly built for long hours of continuous hard work. In addition to the standard model, a number of alternative tipping gears and body styles, both wood and metal, can be supplied to suit many varying conditions of operation.

A Perkins P6 diesel was an option in the 5-tonners at extra cost.

Extras available for the all-steel cab were insulated roof and back panel linings, a heater and a built-in radio.

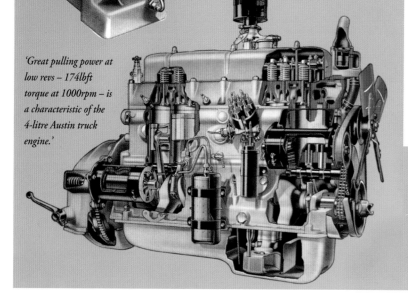

'Great pulling power at low revs – 174lbft torque at 1000rpm – is a characteristic of the 4-litre Austin truck engine.'

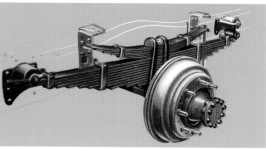

AUSTIN-SCAMMELL

TRACTOR
TRAILER
COMBINATION

TRACTOR
TRAILER
COMBINATION

For payloads of up to 8 tons

The driver was provided with separate handbrake levers for tractor and trailer as well as a release lever for the automatic coupling gear.

The tractor's wheelbase was 9ft 5⁷⁄₁₆in and almost invariably it was fitted with the firm's own 4-litre petrol engine as standard, though a Perkins P6 diesel was an option at increased cost.

The Scammell retractable undercarriage fitted to the front of the trailer. It engaged with the mechanism on the tractor to give instant coupling.

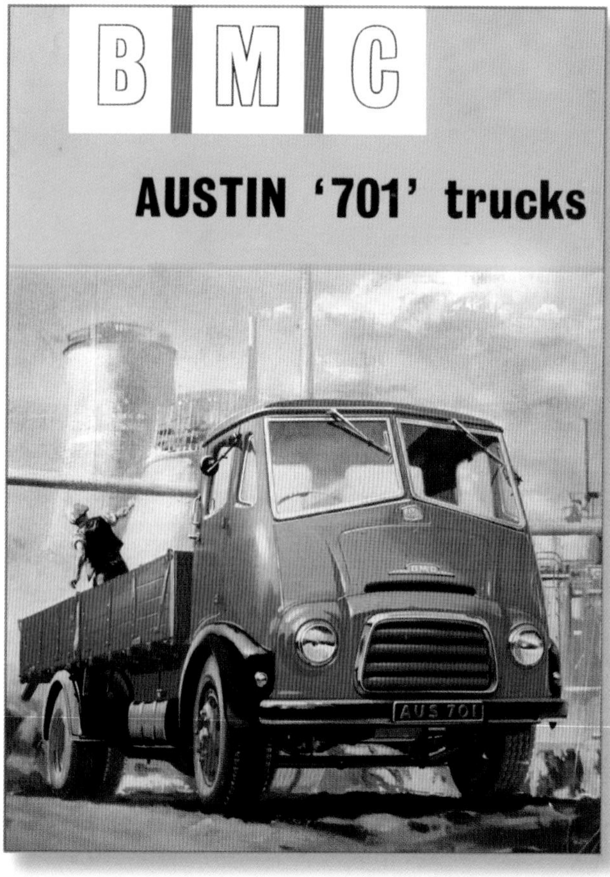

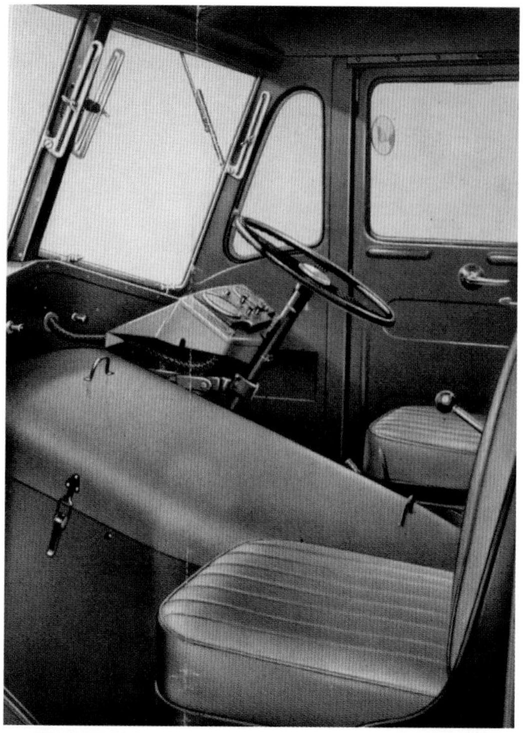

The 701 was of course a bit of BMC badge engineering, and they didn't even bother with different radiator grilles for the Austin and Morris versions. The engine was the BMC 5.1-litre six-cylinder diesel.

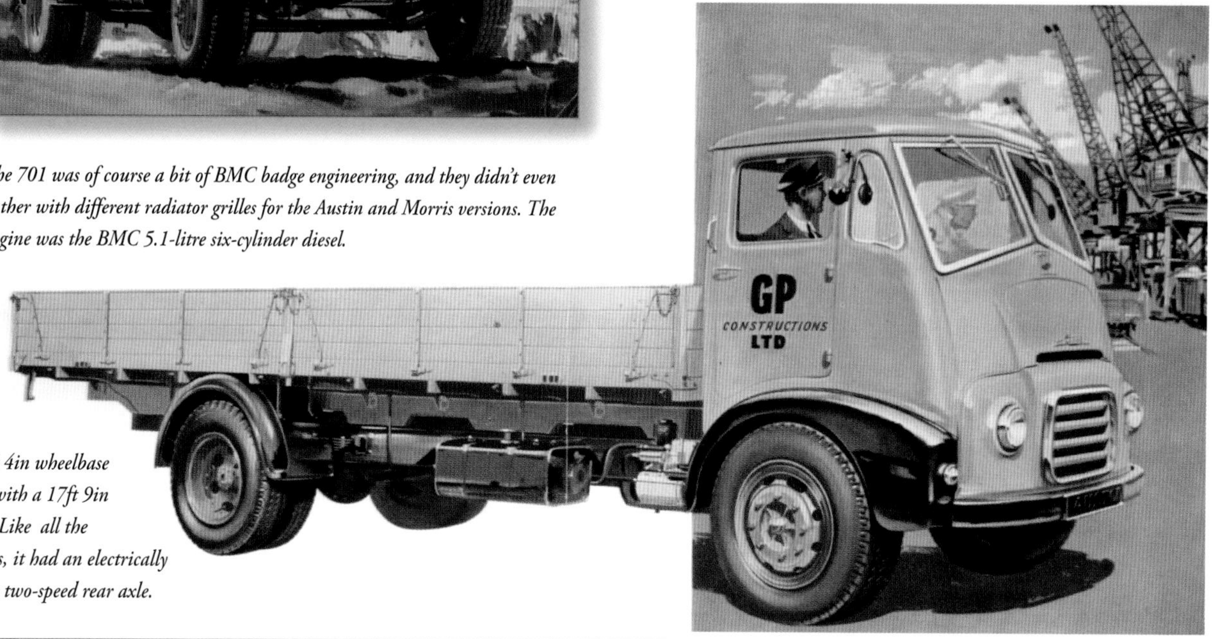

This is the 13ft 4in wheelbase 701 equipped with a 17ft 9in dropside body. Like all the BMC 7-tonners, it had an electrically operated Eaton two-speed rear axle.

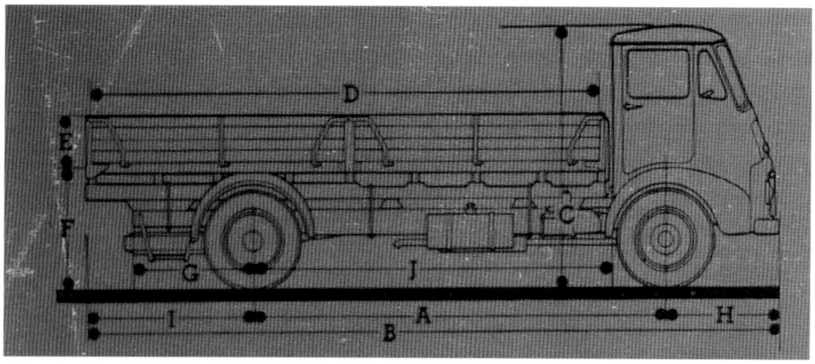

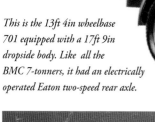

DIMENSIONS		160 in. W.B. Dropside Truck		150 in. W.B. Dropside Truck		120 in. W.B. Chassis/Cab	
		ft. in.	Metres	ft. in.	Metres	ft. in.	Metres
Wheelbase ..	A	13 4	4.06	12 6	3.81	10 0	3.04
Overall Length ..	B	23 8¼	7.22	22 5	6.83	16 2¼	4.93
Overall Height (Laden)	C	8 0⅜	2.44	8 0⅜	2.44	8 0⅜	2.44
Interior Body Length	D	17 9	5.41	16 6	5.03	—	—
Height of Body Sides	E	1 6	0.46	1 6	0.46	—	—
Height of Floor (Laden)	F	3 10	1.17	3 10	1.17	—	—
Rear Hub to End of Frame	G	3 10*	1.17*	3 10	1.17	2 5¾	0.75
Front Hub to Bumper	H	3 8½	1.13	3 8½	1.13	3 8½	1.13
Rear Hub to End of Body	I	6 7¾	2.03	6 2 3/16	1.89	—	—
Rear Hub to Back of Cab	J	11 8	3.56	10 10	3.30	8 4	2.54
Chassis Height (laden) Front		2 5⅝	0.75	2 5⅝	0.75	2 5⅝	0.75
Chassis Height (laden) Rear		2 6¾	0.78	2 6¾	0.78	2 6¾	0.78
Back of Driver's Seat to Centre of Rear Hub ..		11 8	3.56	10 10	3.30	8 4	2.54
Maximum Legal Length behind Driver's Seat ..		18 4	5.59	17 1	5.21	13 4	4.06
Body Interior Width (Max.)		7 0	2.13	7 0	2.13	—	—
Cab Interior Width (Max.)		5 10⅝	1.79	5 10⅝	1.79	5 10⅝	1.79
Overall Width of Vehicle		7 5¾	2.27	7 5¾	2.27	7 5¾	2.27
Track, front		5 10¾	1.80	5 10¾	1.80	5 10¾	1.80
Track, rear		5 8½	1.74	5 8½	1.74	5 8½	1.74
Turning Circle		50 0	15.24	49 6	15.09	42 0	12.80
Ground Clearance ..		8½	0.22	8½	0.22	8½	0.22

Bodywork in primer, as supplied with
Forward Control chassis/scuttle. (Radiator
is left to show position within bodywork
when mounted on chassis.

Bodywork in primer, as
supplied with Normal
Control chassis/scuttle.

The 303 3-tonner had either the 4-litre petrol engine or a BMC 3.4-litre diesel, whereas the 503 5-tonner had the 4-litre petrol or larger 5.1-litre BMC diesel.

Whether 3- or 5-ton, forward or normal control, the vehicle's identity as an Austin or Morris was decided by the front panel incorporating the grille and headlights.

The 303, whether forward control (left) or normal, had an 11ft 6in wheelbase. The 503, however, was available as a tipper with 10ft wheelbase or a truck with one of 13ft 4in.

*A strange brochure
whose cover depicts
the exciting avoidance
of a collision between
a pair of 702s. This
model was little more
than a restyled 701
with virtually the same
chassis and mechanical
specifications.*

*But what is the natty gent pointing out, and
was this improbable and bizarre cab (top right)
specially customized for him? Was it he who so nearly
hit the other truck whilst test driving his new toy?*

*Surely he would have specified the power steering option,
which would have allowed him to make an effortless avoidance.*

Having a wheelbase of only 10 ft. (3·05 m.)
this version only of the Austin '702' truck is fitted
as standard with two speed rear axle. Produced
as a chassis/cab or chassis/scuttle it is ideally
suited to 6 cubic yard (4·59 cu. m.) tipping bodies,
or can be equipped with trailer gear providing
a prime mover for gross train weights of up
to 17 tons (17,272 kg.).

SERIES LD **1 & 1½** TON VANS **AUSTIN**

Austin's version of the Morris LD van

*Opening the rear doors demonstrates a serious design flaw
perpetuated also, it should be said, by other manufacturers
for many years: the poor driver, in the event of an accident
or even upon braking hard, was liable to be assaulted from
the rear by the vehicle's entire load.*

The December 1958 catalogue cover for the 503 and 504 series was virtually a carbon copy of the one for the 503s two years previously, with the new-shape 504 taking the place of the old forward control in the foreground.

In spite of the new look it was the same under the skin, so this 5-tonner has the 13ft 4in wheelbase and is powered by either a 4-litre petrol engine or a 5.1-litre diesel.

What's going on here chaps? It's only the normal-control 303 that has a bench seat and you're in a 304 which has two seats, with either a 3.4-litre diesel or a 4-litre petrol engine between them. Morris marketed this new series as being 'angle designed' but I remember them being referred to colloquially as 'threepenny bit' cab trucks, whether Austin or Morris. Under the Austin name there were other models with the same looks, such as the little 200 with a 9ft 6in wheelbase.

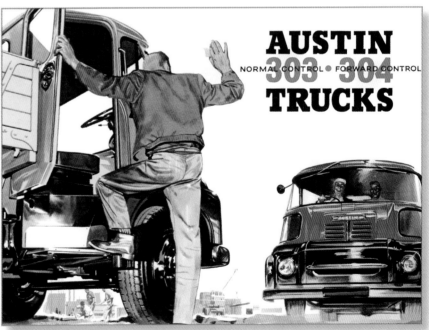

Only two seats in the 404 but the old normal-control had accommodation for three.

Another brochure cover where the participants' activities could be open to conjecture, though I do believe they are only tightening the ropes on the larger 404 'threepenny bit' 4-ton truck while the now old-fashioned looking 403 normal control waits in the background. The latter came with either 11ft 6in or 13ft 4in wheelbase while the 404 had one of 12ft 1in with a choice of the 4-litre petrol or 3.4-litre diesel engine.

Both the '403' Normal and '404' Forward Control 4-tonners are particularly suited for use as bulk-load carriers, or diminishing-load carriers of the delivery-round type. For this purpose, chassis are available equipped with cab or front-end only, to suit the needs of the individual bodybuilder.

The normal-control had been renamed the WE series. The smallest, the K60, had an 11ft 6in wheelbase and either the 3.4-litre BMC diesel or ubiquitous 4-litre petrol engine. The K100 came either as a short-wheelbase 10ft or long-wheelbase 13ft 4in, with 4-litre petrol or 5.1-litre diesel power. The K120 was an export-only variant with a choice of three wheelbases; it was for these only that the 5.7-litre BMC diesel was an option.

Austin WE-K60/K100/K120 Normal Control Trucks are particularly suitable for use as bulk-load carriers, or short-distance carriers of the collection/delivery-round type. The body panels supplied with chassis/scuttle units have been carefully designed to suit the needs of the body-builder, so that he may successfully complete the many types of special body invariably required for this kind of work. Illustrated are some examples of bodywork that are in everyday use. Ranging from refuse collector and cattle truck to tower wagon and horse box, they represent just a few of the many types of body that can be mounted on Austin Normal Control chassis.

The BMC 5.7-litre diesel gave 120bhp at 2500rpm.

In spite of their dated exterior the WEs had an up to the minute cab, but I doubt if they were turned out in these pastel shades.

The FF K140 tipper had a choice of either the 5.1- or 5.7-litre diesel. The wheelbase was 10ft and tipping gear was by under-floor ram by Telehoist (as here) or front ram by Edbro.

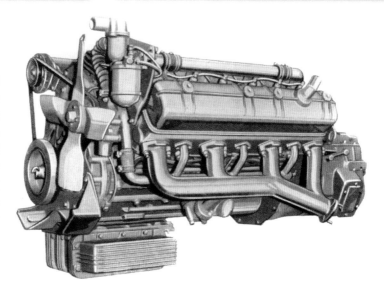

Secret! – until its official unveiling on March 19, 1963. Apart from its under-floor engine with correspondingly more room in the cab, the FH series had, in addition to the wheelbase options of the FF, lengthier versions of 15ft and 17ft 6in.

A new job for the B.M.C. diesel engine! A specially designed sump enables the engine to be inclined for mounting beneath the cab floor. 5·1 litre diesel for FH K100 models—5·7 litre for all FH K140/ K160 trucks. All engines are fitted with hydraulic governors to limit the speed to 2,400 revs. per minute.

BEDFORD

And why not draw attention to the role that you played in the recently concluded hostilities?

When Billy Durant set up General Motors, starting with Buick in 1908 and then in quick succession incorporating Oldsmobile and Cadillac, he surely could not have envisaged that by the mid-1920s the company would be established on mainland Europe and have spread as far afield as, for example, Japan and South Africa.

British operations commenced at the end of 1925 with the acquisition of Vauxhall Motors which, in spite of producing a pair of excellent vehicles in the form of the 14/40 and the legendary 30/98 motor cars, had sunk into a financial quagmire. At first the Americans were content to let the company carry on with the same products but for 1928 their transatlantic thinking was expressed in the first of the GM Vauxhalls, the 20/60.

General Motors' involvement in commercial vehicles had begun in 1911 with the purchase of the Rapid Motor Vehicle Company, one of the more successful truck manufacturers in the US at that time. Since then it had gone on to ingest a good number of other manufacturers, and in Britain by the late 1920s Chevrolet trucks were being built up in North London from imported components. The Vauxhall factory at Luton was being revamped to prepare for large-scale production of the Cadet model, and a decision was taken to extend the facilities still further so that General Motors could embark on the production of its own separate British brand of commercials. It was therefore in 1931 that the first of the Bedfords came into being, a 2-ton truck that was heavily influenced by the GM Chevrolets, it is true, but with a Vauxhall-built motor. From these beginnings the subsequent Bedfords introduced throughout the 1930s became a little more anglicised, with one notable exception. Other British manufacturers, some reluctantly, were turning to diesel power units, but Bedford stuck with its excellent Vauxhall petrol engines until the 1950s.

Just before World War II the first of the 'bull-nosed' Bedfords was introduced, a design which with few modifications was to carry the firm through until well after the war. Anyone old enough to recall the late 1940s and early '50s can surely bring to mind the coach version of the Bedford that offered a means of escape for so many from postwar austerity.

Of all the UK-based manufacturers called upon to supply trucks for the war effort the relatively young firm of Bedford, with its American-rooted mass production capability, outstripped everyone else in the field, and by the time the armistice was signed over a quarter of a million units had been turned out. The company was not idle in other respects either, as amongst its other achievements was the handling of the contract for the Churchill tank from drawing board to production.

Bedford's first entirely new postwar model was the 7-tonner of 1950, still petrol-powered, and the government ordered large numbers of a new four wheel drive 3-ton lorry that had been developed with

IN PEACE OR WAR
You see them everywhere
1939-1945

1945

BEDFORD

The Range of
BEDFORD
VANS, TRUCKS
AND BUSES

Manufactured by
VAUXHALL MOTORS LTD.
Luton, Bedfordshire.

the army in mind. Unlike some other truck manufacturers, Bedford was in a position to expand, and in 1954 a new factory commenced production a few miles away at Dunstable, where, three years later, the 'Big Bedford' range was built. The decision had been made earlier to develop diesel engines, and while this work was under way Perkins diesels were available in Bedford trucks if required. By 1957 Bedford's management was sufficiently confident to start using its own new diesel engines, both four- and six-cylinder, launching them on to the market shortly before the millionth Bedford was completed in 1958.

To some competitors it may have appeared that General Motors' English truck division had a charmed life, and when Bedford came up with the TK in 1960 there must have been many long faces in adversaries' board rooms. The forward-control TK in all its variants was to last for very nearly 20 years and, just as the old 'bull nosed' before it, become a symbol of its age.

Although the company had never previously ventured into the sphere of heavier goods vehicles the success of the TK encouraged management to introduce a larger-capacity version which could carry 12 tons, followed two years later in 1966 by a new 16-ton truck, the KM.

By the mid-1970s the range had been enlarged even further to include rigid lorries up to 24 tons and tractors with a maximum of 32 tons in the UK and later 44 tons for use abroad. The ubiquitous TK was at long last superseded by the next generation in 1980 and one might be excused for imagining that Bedford had an almost limitless life span stretching

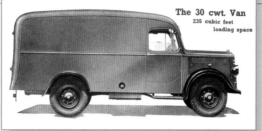

BEDFORD 30 CWT. MODELS

The 30 cwt. Van
235 cubic feet
loading space

Both van and dropside lorry had a wheelbase of 10ft which also served for the shorter 2/3-ton dropside truck. Just one engine served for the entire range, a six-cylinder ohv petrol of 3519cc which produced 72bhp.

The New **Bedford** 10 cubic yard

REFUSE WAGON

with Neville Forward Drive Crew Cab and Eagle Body

ahead of it. But no, for in 1986 General Motors took the decision to cease manufacturing operations in the UK: the Luton plant was closed down and the Dunstable factory was sold off. From then on there were no more Bedfordshire Bedfords and Vauxhalls were made in Germany.

The unusual six-man Neville cab and 10 cubic yard Eagle-bodied refuse wagon came on the market during 1949, warranting its own separate brochure.

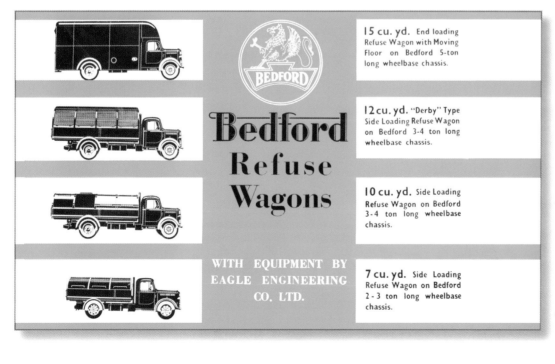

Bedford Refuse Wagons

WITH EQUIPMENT BY
EAGLE ENGINEERING
CO. LTD.

15 cu. yd. End loading Refuse Wagon with Moving Floor on Bedford 5-ton long wheelbase chassis.

12 cu. yd. "Derby" Type Side Loading Refuse Wagon on Bedford 3-4 ton long wheelbase chassis.

10 cu. yd. Side Loading Refuse Wagon on Bedford 3-4 ton long wheelbase chassis.

7 cu. yd. Side Loading Refuse Wagon on Bedford 2-3 ton long wheelbase chassis.

Eagle's regular late-1940s range in conjunction with Bedford. All except the moving floor van type could, at extra cost, be made with removable body to enable the vehicle to be used as an ordinary lorry when required. The 2/3-ton long wheelbase was 11ft 9in, the 3/4-ton long wheelbase 13ft 1in, as on the 5-ton.

A single- to double-deck convertible cattle truck by Spurling was available for the 2/3-, 3/4- and 5-ton chassis, but the use of all Bedfords for general farm duties was also depicted in this 1947 publication.

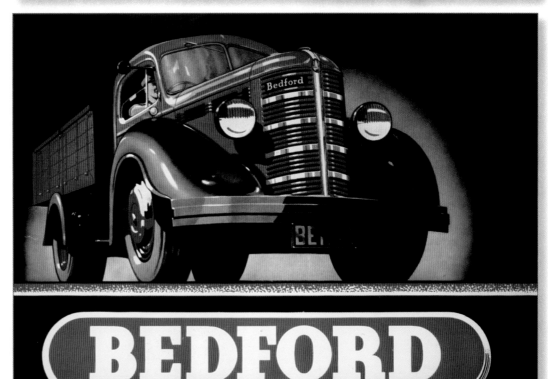

By 1949 model prefixes had come into use. The 30cwts were the K series, the 2/3-ton 10ft-wheelbase was the MS, the 2/3-ton long-wheelbase was the ML, the 3/4-ton long-wheelbase was the OSA, and 5-ton long-wheelbase was the OLB.

All commercials of 30cwt and up were powered by the company's six-cylinder engine.

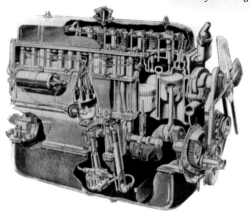

The OSS tractor had a 9ft 3in wheelbase and utilised Scammell automatic coupling gear. This chassis length was also used for the OAS 3/4-ton and OSB 5-ton tippers.

The semi-forward-control cab fitted to the O models.

Bedford Heavy Duty Truck Features

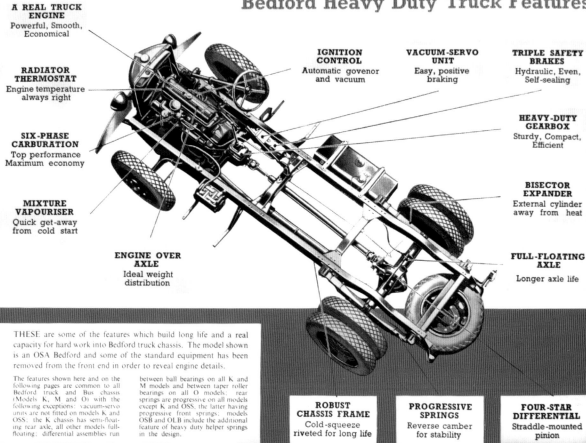

A REAL TRUCK ENGINE
Powerful, Smooth, Economical

RADIATOR THERMOSTAT
Engine temperature always right

SIX-PHASE CARBURATION
Top performance Maximum economy

MIXTURE VAPOURISER
Quick get-away from cold start

ENGINE OVER AXLE
Ideal weight distribution

IGNITION CONTROL
Automatic govenor and vacuum

VACUUM-SERVO UNIT
Easy, positive braking

TRIPLE SAFETY BRAKES
Hydraulic, Even, Self-sealing

HEAVY-DUTY GEARBOX
Sturdy, Compact, Efficient

BISECTOR EXPANDER
External cylinder away from heat

FULL-FLOATING AXLE
Longer axle life

THESE are some of the features which build long life and a real capacity for hard work into Bedford truck chassis. The model shown is an OSA Bedford and some of the standard equipment has been removed from the front end in order to reveal engine details.

The features shown here and on the following pages are common to all Bedford truck and Bus chassis (Models K, M and O) with the following exceptions: vacuum-servo units are not fitted on models K and OSS; the K chassis has semi-floating rear axle, all other models full-floating; differential assemblies run between ball bearings on all K and M models and between taper roller bearings on all O models; rear springs are progressive on all models except K and OSS, the latter having progressive front springs; models OSB and OLB include the additional feature of heavy duty helper springs in the design.

ROBUST CHASSIS FRAME
Cold-squeeze riveted for long life

PROGRESSIVE SPRINGS
Reverse camber for stability

FOUR-STAR DIFFERENTIAL
Straddle-mounted pinion

51

The December 1950 brochure
depicted a large range.

The new forward-controls were christened Big Bedfords and had a
larger 4927cc petrol engine. The tipper had a 9ft 8in wheelbase
and there was a tractor with one of 8ft 2in. In common with other
contemporary Bedfords a four-speed gearbox was employed.

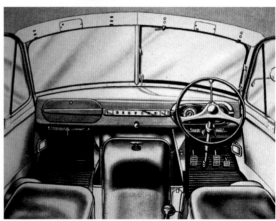

NEW DEAL **BEDFORD** MIDDLEWEIGHT TRUCKS

THE BEST TRUCK VALUE YET!

3-Man Roominess in Cab

Three big men can sit side by side in real comfort in this roomy cab. The total weight of the three men shown in the photograph is 44 stones. The driver is 6 ft. 6 in. tall, and his passengers are also above average height. Even so, there is still plenty of stretching room and head-room.

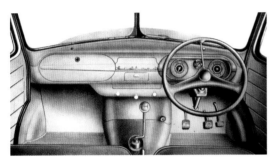

This photo in a 1953 brochure was captioned 'Easy Access means easy maintenance - when there's space to spare – all components are easily accessible'.

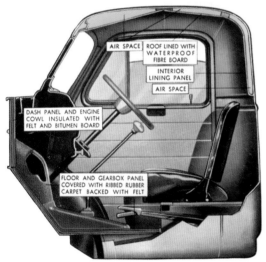

AIR SPACE | ROOF LINED WITH WATERPROOF FIBRE BOARD

INTERIOR LINING PANEL

AIR SPACE

DASH PANEL AND ENGINE COWL INSULATED WITH FELT AND BITUMEN BOARD

FLOOR AND GEARBOX PANEL COVERED WITH RIBBED RUBBER CARPET BACKED WITH FELT

THE A3S & A3L BEDFORDS
3 ton Short and Long Chassis

Wheelbases: 119 in. & 143 in.

Gross Laden Weight 5 tons 5 cwt.

The A4SS tractor had a 10ft wheelbase and was available with the 3½-litre Bedford petrol engine or a Perkins P6V diesel of 4728cc.

A3S and A3L trucks had the 3½-litre petrol engine.

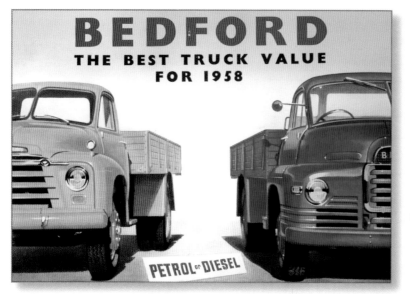

The new Bedford 3284cc four-cylinder diesel for vehicles up to 3-tonners.

Whoops! The artist has gone a little astray here and created the van that never was. This series, however, had a wheelbase of 9ft 11in and either the 214cu in petrol or 200cu in diesel engine.

BEDFORD 25 cwt. and 35 cwt. TRUCKS

WHEELS AND TYRES
4 ton, 7·00 - 20, 10 ply
5 ton, 7·50 - 20, 10 ply
6 ton, 7·50 - 20, 12 ply
For extra heavy duty three-piece wheels are a regular factory option. Tubeless tyres, optional.

EXTRA LONG REAR SPRINGS
50 in. long progressive rear springs, with additional helper springs on 5 and 6 tonners. Extra length gives good riding, light or laden.

LONG LIFE CAB AND SUB-FRAME
Entirely new sub-frame and rubber mountings. Proved on rough track to give longest life ever.

LONG FRONT SPRINGS
45 in. long for good riding and handling qualities on rough sites. Main leaves shot peened for extra life. Angle-set telescopic shock absorbers.

HYPOID AXLE
Entirely new axle. Shafts of larger diameter for longer life. Bedford two-speed axle optional.

RUGGED IN THE RIGHT PLACES

RUGGED FRAME
Extra strength where most needed. High section modulus to withstand heavy impact loads. Cold squeeze riveted for long life.

BIG HYDRAULIC BRAKES PLUS VACUUM-SERVO
Lining area 373 sq. in. plus vacuum servo-assistance, plus the special Bedford tandem hydraulic master cylinder for extra safety. If front brake line is fractured, rear brakes still operate, and vice versa. New moulded brake linings with remarkable anti-fade characteristics.

To account for the strength and toughness of a Bedford you have to know the inside story. It is when you look underneath the chassis that you appreciate the extra value of Bedford engineering and design.

Take a look at this 5-ton tipper. Frame, axles, springs, brakes, cab and sub-frame: all have been engineered to stand up to rough usage. And that goes for all Bedford chassis: they are rugged in the right places!

The 4-, 5- and 6-tonners had a 13ft 9in wheelbase: to power them they had either a 214cu in petrol or 300cu in diesel, the 6-tonner having the additional choice of the larger 300cu in petrol.

Engineered for a gross vehicle weight of 18,000 lb.,* Bedford 4-wheel-drive chassis have all the features for outstanding cross-country mobility . . . large diameter, low pressure tyres for good flotation . . . front and rear wheels tracking for low rolling resistance . . . big ground clearance . . . excellent weight distribution to derive full benefit from 4-wheel drive . . . and the 300 cu. in. petrol engine mated with a 2 to 1 transfer box to deliver power to spare for any gradient.

Designed by the engineers responsible for the famous Bedford QL model which saw war-time service all over the world, the new Bedford 4-wheel-drive models offer go-anywhere cross-country mobility in its most modern form. This Bedford chassis is fully described in a separate catalogue.

Now available also with optional dual rear wheels and heavy-duty springs to raise the g.v.w. to 21,600 lb.

The 300cu in (4927cc) diesel gave 97bhp at 2800rpm.

CROSS COUNTRY 4 x 4 CHASSIS

The 6- and 7-ton dropside trucks had a wheelbase of 13ft with 300cu in petrol or diesel motors, and the 350cu in (5760cc) diesel at extra cost for the 7-tonner if the customer required. All trucks had a four-speed gearbox, with vacuum servo brakes from 2-tonners up.

BEDFORD
Normal control low loaders — 25 cwt. to 4 tons

Some restyling and one-piece windscreens by 1960, except on the Spurling-bodied van but the artist has made a better job of that area this time.

'The new Bedford normal-control cab is the pride and joy of any driver. Note the low step and wide cab doors.'

3-tonners came with a wheelbase of either 9ft 11in or 11ft 11in and 200cu in diesel or 314cu in petrol engines.

Whilst the driver concentrates on the road one of his mates is in a party mood. 'Tried this stuff before?" he asks his apprehensive friend in the cardigan.

When designing this best-ever range of trucks, Bedford engineers set out to increase the driver's range of vision by at least fifty per cent, with particular reference to road vision in the area immediately in front of the cab. The bonnet line is low, and the bonnet slopes away from the driver's line of vision so effectively that his view of the road surface is brought 12 ft. nearer to the cab.

Good thing our driver doesn't smoke or he might have trouble with the multiplicity of obstacles looming up.

The 8-ton tractor unit had a 10ft wheelbase and the good old 214cu in petrol engine or the 300cu in diesel.

Here's the 7-ton tipper with 12ft 11in wheelbase, 300cu in petrol or diesel engine and a two-speed axle as an option.

This was an alternative to the Spurling van on the same 9ft-wheelbase 25cwt and 35cwt chassis.

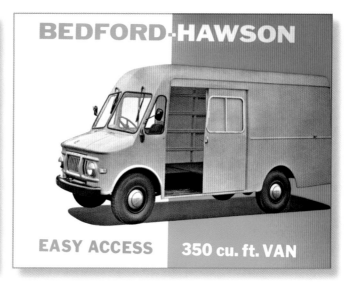

BEDFORD-HAWSON

EASY ACCESS 350 cu. ft. VAN

That other motoring icon, the Mini, was but one year old when Bedford's TK first hit the road in 1960. It did not offer any radical mechanical departures from what had gone before but was just a thoroughly well thought out design. The standard truck was made as a 3-, 4- or 5-tonner with an 11ft 3in wheelbase, as a 5-, 6- or 7-tonner with one of 12ft 7in, and as a 7- or 7½-tonner with one of 13ft 11in. Engines ranged from the 214cu in petrol to the 350cu in diesel depending on model.

Despite the jazzy, contemporary interior the seats were not particularly comfortable on a long run but it was a relief to be in a forward-control that didn't have the motor in the cab with you. A five-speed box was standard on everything from 6-tonners up unless your 6-tonner had the 214 petrol motor, in which case you had a four-speed like the smaller TKs.

BEDFORD

NEW FORWARD CONTROL **TK** TRUCKS

The TK cab is designed for easy removal. A skilled team can lift the cab clear in about 30 minutes. Normal maintenance is effected through the hinged flaps, with the cab in situ.

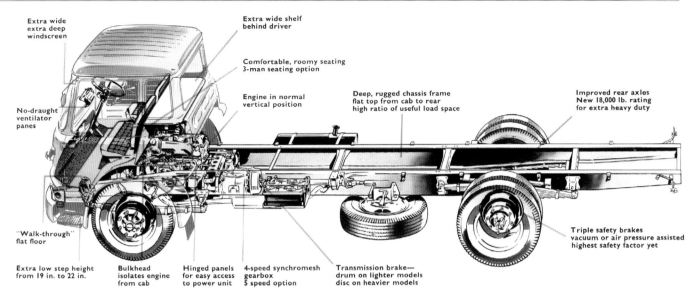

Extra wide
extra deep
windscreen

No-draught
ventilator
panes

"Walk-through"
flat floor

Extra wide shelf
behind driver

Comfortable, roomy seating
3-man seating option

Engine in normal
vertical position

Deep, rugged chassis frame
flat top from cab to rear
high ratio of useful load space

Improved rear axles
New 18,000 lb. rating
for extra heavy duty

Triple safety brakes
vacuum or air pressure assisted
highest safety factor yet

Extra low step height
from 19 in. to 22 in.

Bulkhead
isolates engine
from cab

Hinged panels
for easy access
to power unit

4-speed synchromesh
gearbox
5 speed option

Transmission brake—
drum on lighter models
disc on heavier models

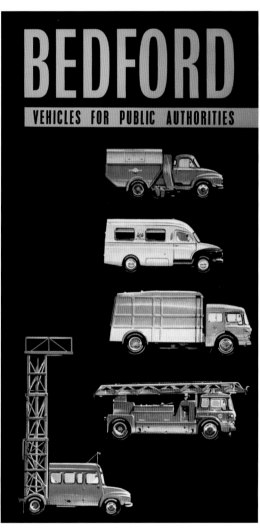

BEDFORD
VEHICLES FOR PUBLIC AUTHORITIES

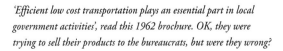

'Efficient low cost transportation plays an essential part in local government activities', read this 1962 brochure. OK, they were trying to sell their products to the bureaucrats, but were they wrong?

A 'Yorkshire' 1000-gallon cesspit emptier.

Firefighting vehicle by Pyrene.

A tower and workshop by Eagle.

There were four variants of the 8ft wheelbase tractor unit, 8-, 10- and 12-ton plus the HD (Heavy Duty) which was new for 1962. All HDs had the big 400cu in Bedford diesel as standard. The 12-ton and HD had a two-speed axle but this was optional on the smaller capacity models.

Bedford chose a rather more trendy driver to model the TK's cab but our friends from the 1950s were still hard at it promoting the forward control's cabs elsewhere in this 1962 brochure.

Tippers all had a 10ft wheelbase and the 300cu in petrol, or by this time (1963) had either a 330cu in or a 370cu in diesel unless the vehicle was an HD.

Engine compartment was illuminated by two lamps so that 'All routine maintenance jobs can be carried out with the utmost facility'.

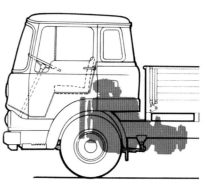

Bedford's largest diesel displaced 400cu in (6540cc) and developed 131bhp at 2400rpm, with 317lb ft of torque at 1600rpm.

Extra long 7- or 7½-ton bulk loaders had a 13ft 11in wheelbase and either a 300cu in petrol or a 330cu in diesel, with the 370cu in diesel optional for the 7½-tonner.

COMMER

Commer's initial postwar restyling exercise resulted in a frontal aspect that was a melange of Rootes Humbers and Hillmans. Wheelbase was either 10ft 2in or 12ft 11in and, a six-cylinder ohv 4139cc petrol engine was fitted (later it went into the Humber Super Snipe IV). Gearbox was a four-speed and brakes Girling hydraulic.

lthough initially based in London, the firm Commercial Cars, founded in 1905, very soon moved out of the metropolis to Luton and began to manufacture lorries for both home and export markets. By the time World War I began it had sufficient standing to be awarded government contracts which entailed the building of some 3000 trucks between 1914 and 1918. However, in the conditions prevailing immediately after the war momentum was lost, and the firm hovered on the brink of insolvency until bought by Humber during 1926. The new owners abbreviated the name to simply Commer and at the same time started to build a fresh range of commercials of up to 4½-ton capacity, as well as passenger chassis, but within two years Humber itself had been absorbed into the burgeoning Rootes empire.

For Rootes the Commer acquisition provided a base from which to go into the large-scale production of reasonably-priced commercials. The first of these

was to be the Humber Snipe-engined 2-ton Invader of 1929, which was shortly joined by a 6-tonner also with a six-cylinder petrol engine. In 1932 Commer became the first commercial vehicle firm to use Perkins diesel engines in its products, at a time when many others, in the early years of widespread acceptance of this fuel, preferred motors by the likes of Gardner.

Throughout the remaining years of the 1930s Commer's medium and heavyweight commercials were known as the LN series, but during the year war was declared in Europe these were superseded by the Q, more commonly known as Superpoise, range.

The Ministry of Supply kept the firm busy during the war period and something over 25,000 trucks rolled out of the factory, together with munitions and a large number of Humber armoured cars.

It was not until 1948 that a completely new design was introduced, in the form of an under-floor engined lorry that could meet many of the various requirements

THE COMMER 2-3 TON 'SUPERPOISE' MODEL

with six-cylinder o.h.v. engine developing 85 b.h.p.

of the road haulage trade. From 1954, as a result of Rootes takeover of the Tilling Stevens company in 1951, the wonderful supercharged two-stroke diesel engine which Tilling Stevens had been developing was fitted into these. This range, along with updated versions of the bonneted Superpoise trucks, continued to be produced throughout the 1950s, with periodic updates when fashion dictated or, in the case of one-piece windscreens, when improved manufacturing processes allowed.

At the beginning of the 1960s a medium-weight multi-stop delivery vehicle, of American influence, was brought out, capable of payloads from 1½ to 3 tons. This was badged as a Karrier, a firm that Rootes had acquired before the war, and later as a Dodge in years to come. During the same period, in answer to Bedford's recently introduced and immensely successful TK range, further modernisation of the truck range took place and a larger-capacity four-wheeler, the Maxiload, joined the family.

Chrysler had had intentions towards Rootes for some while and in 1964 became the majority share-holders, which meant that henceforth Commer, along with its subsidiary Karrier, would become ever more entwined with Chrysler's Dodge commercials. Some Dodges became Commers or even Karriers, if for municipal duties, but in the mid-1970s Chrysler decided to concentrate on one identity, to phase out the Commer brand entirely and to call all their British commercials Dodge.

THE COMMER WITH 'UNDER-FLOOR' ENGINE
5 and 7 Tonners

IMPROVED VISIBILITY

Seated fully forward the driver has a wide and unrestricted view of the road through the two-piece wide vision windscreen with dual wipers.

Artist Terence Cuneo was commissioned to produce a painting for the cover of this 1950 brochure.

A 6½- to 7-ton tipper was also listed, with a 9ft 7in wheelbase. Standard tipping gear was under-body Telehoist equipment with the hydraulic pump driven off the gearbox.

Illustrated is the 11' 9" w.b. dropsider with 15' 6" × 6' 10" × 1' 6" body. In the case of the 13' 6" w.b. model, body length is increased to 18' 0".

AN OUTSTANDING DESIGN AFFORDING GREATER POWER — INCREASED DRIVER
COMFORT AND VISIBILITY — IMPROVED MANOEUVRABILITY — LONGER LIFE —

The 4.1-litre petrol engine was bored out to 4750cc and modified so that it would happily run on its side, and at the same time produce 109bhp, in order to slot it in under the floor of the forward-control Commers.

By the early 1950s the Superpoise could be had in many guises: 5-ton tipper, 8- to 10-ton tractor, ambulance, and trucks up to 5 tons. The forward-control was also available to fulfil a variety of roles: its tractor could cope with 10-12 tons and, along with the larger Superpoise tractor had a two-speed rear axle.

'The layout of the cab and its fittings are more in keeping with a luxury car than a truck', read the brochure, which may explain why a pair of ghostly refugees from a country club have spirited themselves into the vehicle to take a 'luxury' ride with the phantom trucker.

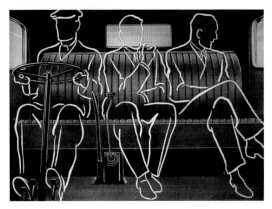

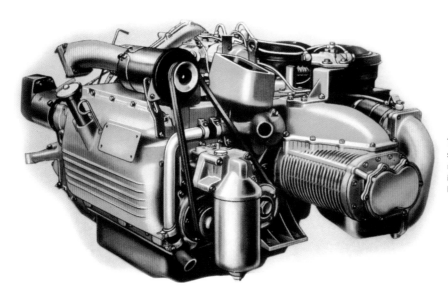

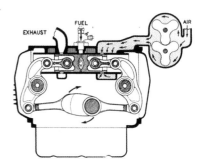

1. Exhaust and inlet ports are sealed by pistons as they approach mean inner dead centre. Fuel is then injected into the cylinder and combustion takes place.

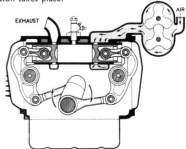

2. The high pressures generated by combustion force the pistons outwards on their working stroke, so actuating the linkage to turn the crankshaft.

In all the sales literature that I have come across the only hint of the origins of this engine, which Rootes called their own, is in its title, the TS3, although the prefix might equally well stand for two-stroke. Be that as it may, the engine had been under development by the Tilling Stevens/Vulcan combine in the late 1940s before they were absorbed by Rootes and was indeed manufactured in their factory at Maidstone in Kent.

I make no excuses for devoting a whole page to this fascinating two-stroke, opposed-piston, supercharged diesel motor, which gave the Commer lorries into which it was fitted such a distinctive sound. Its vital statistics were a bore of 82.55mm and stroke of 101.6mm which gave a capacity of 3261cc in its three cylinders, in each of which were two cast iron pistons with steel heat-resisting crowns. It put out 105bhp at 2400rpm and the excellent torque figure of 270lb ft at 1200rpm. The Roots-type supercharger was manufactured by Wade and, interestingly, many have been given a new lease of life, when fitted with different seals to cope with petrol, as superchargers for pre-war cars and hot rods.

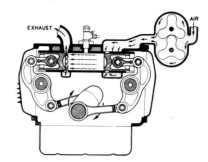

3. Towards the end of the working stroke the phasing of the pistons enables the exhaust ports to open before the inlet. The design of the exhaust ports is such that burnt gases are rapidly expelled from the cylinder into the exhaust system.

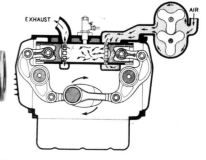

4. Shortly afterwards the inlet ports are uncovered and air, supplied to the air chest via the blower unit, rushes into the cylinder, sweeping remaining exhaust gases out through the exhaust ports.

Commer forward-control tractor, shown coupled to
a machinery drop-frame semi-trailer.

The artic had a 7ft 10in wheelbase whether it was the 10 to11- or 12-ton version. The former had an overdrive option for its four-speed gearbox, while the latter had a five-speed box and Eaton two-speed axle by 1955. Power brakes and steering were also an option on the 12-tonner but both came with either the 4.1-litre petrol engine or the Rootes two-stroke diesel.

This 1958 brochure illustrates the new one-piece windscreen and yet another face lift for the radiator grille. All was much the same otherwise, with the five-model range of two artics, two trucks with either the 11ft 9in or 13ft 6in wheelbase, and a tipper.

COMMER

7 TON TRUCKS and 10-11 & 12 TON TRACTORS

PETROL OR DIESEL   ROOTES PRODUCTS

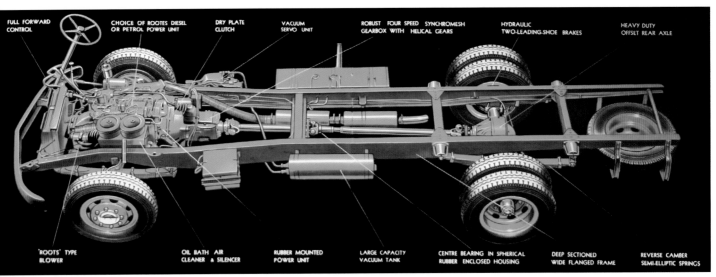

FULL FORWARD CONTROL

CHOICE OF ROOTES DIESEL OR PETROL POWER UNIT

DRY PLATE CLUTCH

VACUUM SERVO UNIT

ROBUST FOUR SPEED SYNCHROMESH GEARBOX WITH HELICAL GEARS

HYDRAULIC TWO-LEADING-SHOE BRAKES

HEAVY DUTY OFFSET REAR AXLE

'ROOTS' TYPE BLOWER

OIL BATH AIR CLEANER & SILENCER

RUBBER MOUNTED POWER UNIT

LARGE CAPACITY VACUUM TANK

CENTRE BEARING IN SPHERICAL RUBBER ENCLOSED HOUSING

DEEP SECTIONED WIDE FLANGED FRAME

REVERSE CAMBER SEMI-ELLIPTIC SPRINGS

COMMER

'SUPERPOISE' 2-3, 3-4, 5 and 6 TON MODELS

PETROL OR DIESEL   ROOTES PRODUCTS

The Superpoise of 1961 had a 10ft 2in or 13ft 1in wheelbase for all models up to 4 tons, 12ft for the 5-ton tipper, and 14ft 1in for the 5- and 6-tonners. Engines were the 4.1 petrol or a Perkins P6 diesel, with the larger Perkins Six-354 of 5800cc for the 5- and 6-tonners, which also had the option of a two-speed axle unless fitted with overdrive.

The Commer six-point rubber-mounted cab. Forward-controls had a similar system but with four points.

The Commer 1½-ton F.C was also marketed as the Karrier Cruiser, with petrol or diesel power and a wheelbase of 10ft 3in. This one was happily running around Ceylon (Sri Lanka) making deliveries of cough medicine for Gargills.

NEW COMMER 'WALK-THRU'
RANGE OF 1½ • 2 AND 3 TONNERS, PETROL OR DIESEL

With cowl in driving compartment removed, rear of engine can be serviced with ease.

The Walk Thru was brought out in 1961. Smaller versions had the same wheelbase as the previous FC 1½-ton van. The wheelbase was 11ft 1in on the 3-ton and this was also an option on the 2-ton models. 1½- and 2-tonners had either the 2266cc four-cylinder Humber Hawk ohv motor or the new Humber Super Snipe 2965cc six-cylinder. For those who preferred a diesel a four-cylinder unit of 2260cc was available. The 3-ton van had either the Snipe motor or a Perkins Four-203 of 3330cc.

Handbrake was mounted on the steering column.

Cab versions had concertina doors.

An extremely low stepwell enables entrance to be made with little more than normal walking effort.

Driver approaches his seat automatically, without any fumbling or clambering.

Instinctively, and without further trouble or obstruction, he takes his seat.

Now seated, the driver relaxes with hands and feet naturally in position.

COMMER 10-11 & 12 TON TRACTORS

with new extra-wide luxury cab affording superb driver comfort

* **Extra wide doors for ease of access**

* **Low step height**

* **Powered by the famous Rootes diesel engine**

* **Power-assisted hydraulic brakes**

* **Available with "Scammell" Automatic or 'Fifth-wheel' coupling gear**

Backed by Country-wide Parts and Service Organisation

For 1962 there was a brand new cab for the big forward-controls and an additional 8-tonner in either tipper form, with regular wheelbase of 9ft 7in, or truck form, the latter having a considerably longer wheelbase of 15ft 7in. They were all powered by the TS.35 motor.

In 1963 the truck range was re-engined and marketed as follows – The 4-tonner (11ft 9in wheelbase) had either the old 4.1-litre six-cylinder petrol engine or a six-cylinder diesel of 3860cc. The 5-tonner (11ft 9in wheelbase or 9ft 7in wheelbase tipper) had the same or a larger diesel six of 5800cc, as did the 11ft 9in wheelbase 6-tonner, with a further choice of the bored-out six-cylinder petrol engine (both petrol engines now reverting to their original form and running upright). The 7-tonners all had the Perkins 6.354 motor.

The new cab could also be ordered in double-cab form with an additional rear compartment which had a rear-facing bench seat for four crew, but this was an unusual format and the interior normally looked like this.

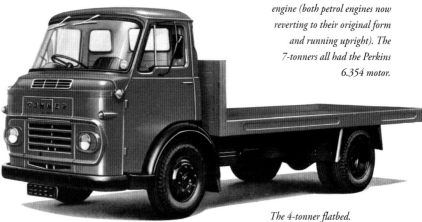

The 4-tonner flatbed.

POWER UNIT ACCESSIBILITY

Cab design is such that complete and easy frontal access to the power unit is made possible by removing the large grille panel. Engine removal is simplicity itself. After removing front bumper, front chassis crossmember and radiator assembly, the engine and its ancillary components can be withdrawn with the greatest of ease. Installation is equally simple, the sequence of operations being merely reversed.

DENNIS

In 1899 two brothers, John and Raymond Dennis, set up a business at Guildford in Surrey in order to manufacture bicycles, motorcycles and motor cars. Early on they gave these the evocative title of Speed King, which was maybe a little premature, but within a few years the marque did accrue one or two mild competition successes – after this title had been dropped. The firm's real forte proved to be solid, reliable touring cars, but the first steps towards commercial vehicle manufacture had been made during 1904 as a result of a request from Tilling, the bus company, to supply a running chassis. In the years leading up to the First World War the business expanded quite rapidly as

more work of this nature came in: the first Dennis fire engine was built and light and medium trucks were in production.

So successful had the commercial side of the business become by 1914 that the decision was taken to abandon the manufacture of cars. Any prospect of a reduction in business as a result was negated by essential war work, coupled with government orders for several thousand of the 4-ton A-type trucks. After four very profitable years Dennis celebrated by buying the engine manufacturing company of White & Poppe in 1919. In the early 1920s, to further add to its repertoire, it started designing and producing specialised municipal vehicles.

With the Depression just around the corner the firm came up with some advanced passenger vehicles but these were not sufficiently powerful to break the virtual duopoly that Leyland and AEC had in that sphere. Dennis's strength was in its fire appliances and municipal vehicles and it was those that enabled the company to weather the early 1930s, which brought down so many firms. Strangely, in spite of having its own engine factory, Dennis resisted the switch to diesel power which took place in those years, and when it did finally succumb to fashion it was several years later and by way of the products of Perkins and Gardner.

In the years that remained before the next war engulfed Europe Dennis re-entered the passenger vehicle arena, with single-deckers only, as well as offering a greater variety of trucks encompassing payloads from 2 to 12 tons.

From 1939 to 1945, along with the rest of the motor industry, government contracts were the order of the day, and in Dennis's case this meant Bren gun carriers, Churchill tanks and all wheel driven trucks, as well as military versions of the 12-tonners.

The war over, the company was quicker than many to announce new models, although to be frank whoever came up with the look of the Horla tractor units was anything but an aesthete. Be that as it may, they were designed to do a job of work and were soon joined by both six- and eight-wheeler trucks and passenger chassis, all utilising in-house diesel engines. Throughout the 1950s the firm continued to develop and produce a

'By Appointment to the late King George V' was the proud statement on this 1947 brochure, which depicted a comforting rural idyll after the war years, but is this a pub that is taking a copious beer delivery?

THE

DENNIS

"PAX" Chassis

N.-C. or F.-C.

for

5-TON LOADS

"It's best carried by Dennis."

BY APPOINTMENT
MOTOR VEHICLE
MANUFACTURERS
TO THE LATE
KING GEORGE V

DENNIS Bros., Ltd.
GUILDFORD, ENGLAND

Phone : Guildford 5291
Grams : Dennis, Guildford

Whether forward- or normal-control, the Pax had wheelbase options as follows: 9ft 6in, 11ft 6in or 12ft 10in. An NC tipper was made using either of the shorter two. The engine was a four-cylinder sidevalve of 3770cc which produced 70bhp, and the gearbox was a four-speed. The manufacturer's prose contained some lovely pieces such as 'Of the Dennis Pax 5-tonner it is truly said, "Handsome is and handsome does"'.

range of specialised fire-fighting and municipal vehicles, alongside bus chassis and some rather lacklustre lorries, but towards the end of the decade it brought out the first of several types of large delivery vans that were to be offered in the coming years. Although ahead of their time in some respects, these were not a huge success; neither were the heavier lorries that Dennis was now making as the 1960s unfolded, and one cannot help but feel that the company would have been far better off concentrating on what it had proved it could do best. Little did the management know it, but within just a few years its other markets would have evaporated. From that time and until Dennis was bought by the Hestair Group in 1972, its emergency vehicles and, to use an Americanism, garbage trucks would be its only source of income.

Strangely, for a very short time after the takeover, Dennis-badged trucks were built up from exported components in Cyprus by a firm named KMC.

The Hestair Dennis combine is known nowadays as Dennis Specialist Vehicles and continues to make the types of vehicles for which it became renowned nearly a lifetime ago.

Many Dennis vehicles serve the United Dairies Ltd.— this normal-control Pax has a platform body with detachable stanchions and chains.

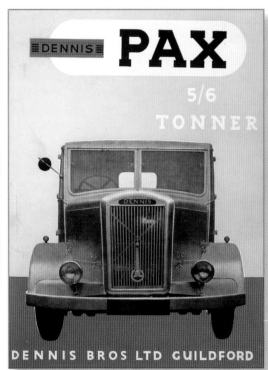

The Pax II had the capability of a greater head of steam if you opted for the overhead-valve version of the old sidevalve motor, which gave out an extra 10bhp. Maybe an even better choice could have been to go for a diesel, which meant a Perkins P6, in which case Dennis would allow you to have a five-speed gearbox as well if you asked. Another option on this latest Pax was servo assistance for the hydraulic brakes.

The forward-control chassis.

The 3770cc sidevalve engine had a bore and stroke of 100mm by 120mm, which it shared with the ohv motor.

The JUBILANT

FOR 12 TON LOADS

DENNIS
BROS LTD
GUILDFORD

BY APPOINTMENT
MOTOR VEHICLE
MANUFACTURERS
TO THE LATE
KING GEORGE V

The Dennis 0.6 diesel of 1951 put out around 100bhp at 1800rpm; later versions managed nearer 120bhp.

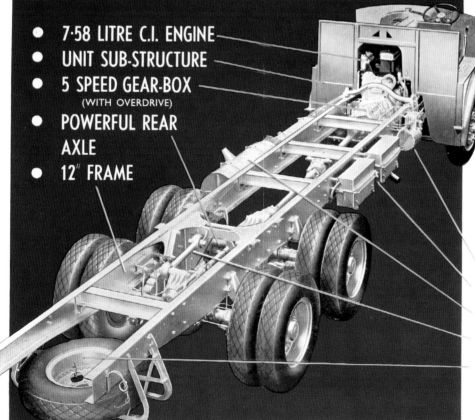

- 7·58 LITRE C.I. ENGINE
- UNIT SUB-STRUCTURE
- 5 SPEED GEAR-BOX
  (WITH OVERDRIVE)
- POWERFUL REAR
  AXLE
- 12" FRAME

Wheelbase of the Jubilant was 17ft 10½in. An auxiliary two-speed gearbox could be fitted as an optional extra.

- HYDRAULIC & SERVO BRAKING
- 24 VOLT-STARTING & CHARGING
- 44 GALLON FUEL TANK
- RUBBER CUSHIONED DRIVE
- 24 FOOT BODY SPACE

I'm sorry but I have to be frank here and caption this 'another hideous vehicle from Dennis'. Perhaps on the other hand they were good to drive, although the performance cannot have been startling if you went for the cheapest engine option of the three, which was the same 70bhp unit as on the Pax II. Trailer coupling gear was the Scammell system.

DENNIS HORLA

FOR SEMI TRAILERS OPERATING AT 12 TONS GROSS

PUBLICATION NUMBER 249C

DENNIS BROS LTD GUILDFORD

DENNIS UNITED Max

more miles with a Max

The Max was a much better looking beast and in its four-cylinder form was powered by the 6.5-litre Dennis 0.4 ohv diesel, which had four valves per cylinder.
The Dennis four-speed gearbox had a preselective overdrive fifth speed which allowed a clutchless change to this highest ratio.

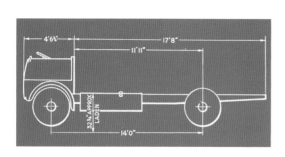

The old-established brewery Fremlins was a good customer of Dennis, as this 1951 brochure shows. Although Fremlins was absorbed by Whitbread many years ago and is now extinct, the Dennis name lives on.

The Max 6 was powered by the Dennis four-valve 0.6 diesel of 7.58 litres and used the Dennis overdrive 4/5 speed gearbox. The truck had a 15ft 6in wheelbase, the tipper one of 10ft 11in and the tractor 9ft 6in.

Quaint is most probably the kindest way to describe the late 1950s Heron. This dumpy little 3-tonner was powered by the 3.14-litre Perkins P4, which gave 55bhp and was coupled to a four-speed gearbox. The cab could be all-steel or wood-framed with aluminium panelling. The makers were at least confident, or appeared so from their catalogue description, 'Imposing new styling'!

DENNIS

HERON

sturdy, reliable, efficient & economical

LIGHTWEIGHT DIESEL CHASSIS

DENNIS BROS LTD GUILDFORD

The Pax IV of 1961 came with any of the following six-cylinder diesel motors: a 5.1-litre BMC, 5-litre Perkins 305 or 5.8-litre Perkins 354, with a choice of four- or five-speed gearbox. By this time Dennis brochures were cheaply produced and as unattractive as the company's products, but they read hopefully – 'a particularly attractive investment where specialist bodywork is contemplated'. In all probability the most successful version was just such a thing, in the shape of the Paxit refuse collection vehicle.

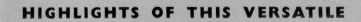

HIGHLIGHTS OF THIS VERSATILE **PAX IV CHASSIS**

RESTYLED ROOMY CAB
LARGE ONE PIECE WINDSCREEN
GLASS FIBRE BONNET TOP
DOUBLE SKIN ROOF

FOR LONG DISTANCE SERVICE OR LOCAL DELIVERY WORK...

POWERFUL BRAKES
PAIRED HEADLAMPS
SUPERB STEERING
WIDE RANGE OF WHEELBASES

DODGE

The seven-model range for 1949 included this van, which shared the same 11ft 9in wheelbase as the 2/3-ton lorry and had a six-cylinder 109bhp petrol engine. This chassis was known as the Model 64.

Since 1931 the Chrysler Corporation's Dodge trucks, which had been imported and assembled in England for some years, had been losing ground to their rivals from across the Atlantic, General Motors. GM had made a shrewd move when it founded Bedford, which would carry none of the stigma attached to imports during the Depression and could offer work when so many of the population were unemployed. Consequently, during 1933, but without going the whole hog and starting a fresh brand name, Chrysler commenced the actual manufacture of trucks at its English headquarters at Kew in Surrey. At first the new 'British' Dodge range, which still used engines and transmissions manufactured in the US, consisted of a couple of trucks, the larger one capable of carrying just two tons. Gradually, however, the identity, if not the name, became less transatlantic, and within three years the range had been enlarged to include forward-control flatbeds and tippers of double the original capacity. The following year saw further changes and in 1938 diesel engines, by Perkins, began to be offered as an alternative power unit, something which Dodge's GM rivals were to put off until well after the war.

The first of the new post war-Dodges, from 2- to 6-tonners, were unmistakably rehashed from the late 1930s range, and customers had to wait until 1949 for more modern styling; even then it was uncannily like some contemporary Leylands.

The firm's lack of original thinking continued through the 1950s and by the latter part of the decade the forward-control had a cab shared with Leyland,

DODGE DELIVERY VAN. Available on 2/3 ton chassis only. It has a distinctly modern appearance and a load capacity of 450 cu. ft.

and the normal-control models shared theirs with the Commer Superpoise.

Dodge had yet to venture into the heavy classes, the range circa 1962 encompassing forward-control trucks up to 9 tons and bonneted up to 7 tons. A year or so later the latter were given American styling for a while, just before the Chrysler/Rootes tie-up of 1964. In this set-up Chrysler held the purse strings and called the shots, one consequence being that Dodge

gradually became the dominant commercial brand and Commer began its slide into oblivion.

As a result of all this the Kew factory closed in 1967, production moving to the Commer site at Dunstable. By the following year 24-tonners carrying the Dodge name were on sale, extending Dodge's share of the market still further. From 1976 all commercials produced by the combine, with the exception of some Karriers, were Dodges.

The choice remained the same for 1951. Dodge, from its early days of building vehicles in the UK, drove home the message that these were local as opposed to imported products.

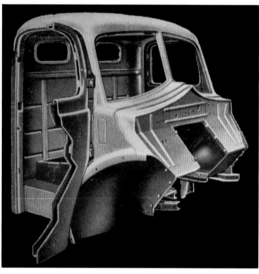

Cabs were of all-steel welded construction.

DODGE CHASSIS ARE BUILT TO DO THE TOUGHEST JOBS

The 13ft 9in wheelbase chassis illustrated here was known as the Model 105; it was also available with a Perkins P6 engine. The shorter 5-tonner (9ft 11in wheelbase) had a tipper body and could be had as a diesel or petrol. The largest in the range was a six-tonner which had a slightly more powerful (114bhp) petrol engine and was made as a long-wheelbase lorry (Model 125) or short-wheelbase tipper (Model 123).

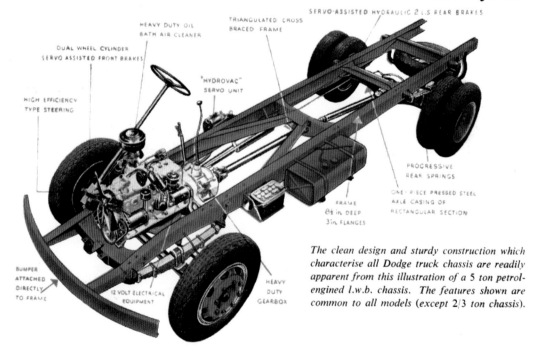

The clean design and sturdy construction which characterise all Dodge truck chassis are readily apparent from this illustration of a 5 ton petrol-engined l.w.b. chassis. The features shown are common to all models (except 2/3 ton chassis).

Any of the chassis could be adapted for specialised purposes or bodywork.

A 2,000 galion semi-trailer tanker coupled to a Dodge 6 ton 9 ft. 11 in. w.b. chassis.

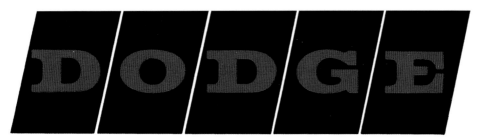

HEAVY DUTY DUMP TRUCK

The 1959 Dodge dump truck, with link tip gear and 6 cubic yard body by Telehoist, was built on the 9ft 8⅜in wheelbase chassis. There were two catalogued models, the only difference being the engine: the 3144DBR had a 5.56-litre six-cylinder diesel engine and the 3144 DBY had a slightly larger 5.76-litre unit; both had a five-speed gearbox.

From their inception in 1958 Dodge forward-control chassis, as well as being marketed with standard dropside truck and pick up bodies, were used for many purposes which entailed the use of specialised bodywork.

This 8-tonner of 1960, in common with other Dodges of the period, had a bewildering number of sub-models. The shorter-wheelbase 3165Y had a 5.76-litre engine, the 3265T a 5.8-litre and the 3165AZ one of 6.17 litres; all were six-cylinder diesels. The long-wheelbase was known as the 3166 and had the same suffixes relating to engine size. All had five-speed gearboxes and the AZs had two-speed rear axles.

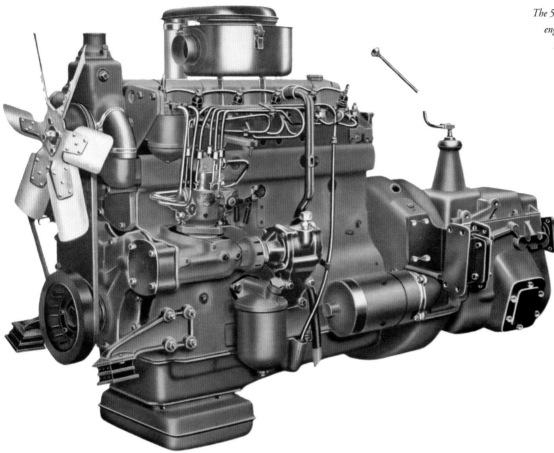

The 5.8-litre six-cylinder diesel engine developed 112bhp at 2800rpm and 260lb ft of torque at 1450rpm.

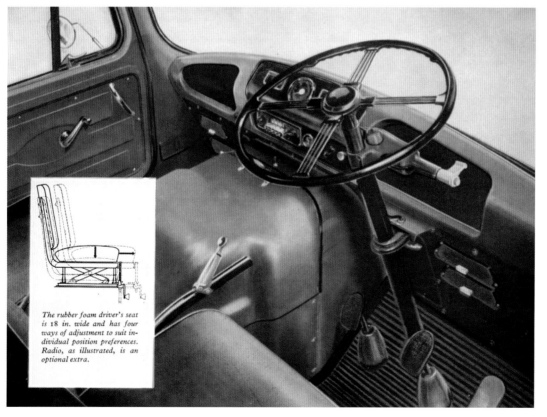

The rubber foam driver's seat is 18 in. wide and has four ways of adjustment to suit individual position preferences. Radio, as illustrated, is an optional extra.

Visibility seemed to be constantly on the minds of the manufacturers, and Dodge's sales piece here was 'Luxury cab with "pilot house" visibility'. Potential purchasers were, I am sure, very interested to note that the wrap-around windscreen had a rake of 18 degrees and the generous glass area of 1512sq in.

This vehicle is decked out with all the bits and pieces that were offered as extras, such as radio, heater, flashing indicators and windscreen washers. The cab body was of all-steel welded construction and was rubber mounted at four points.

TRACTOR MODELS

D308 — Nominal Payload Rating 12 tons
Max. G.C.W. 40,500 lb. (18,371 kgs.)

D309 — Nominal Payload Rating 14 tons
Max. G.C.W. 45,000 lb. (20,412 kgs.)

These tractors had a wheelbase of 8ft 4in. The 308 had the 5.8-litre motor with the 6.1-litre as an option, whilst the 309 had the 6.7 unit. All had five-speed gearboxes and two-speed axles. The 308 had vacuum servo assistance for the brakes and the 309 had air. Lorry manufacturers were a mean lot and were still listing flashing direction indicators as an optional extra – this was 1963 and even the humble Mini had had them as standard since its launch in 1959!

DODGE

12 TON TRACTOR

WITH AUTOMATIC COUPLING

MODEL D307 s.w.b.

Nominal Payload Rating 7 tons
Max. G.V.W. 23,000 lb. (10,433 kgs.)
Max. G.C.W. 40,500 lb.* (18,371 kgs.)
* with standard engine max. G.C.W. is 35,000 lb. (15,876 kgs.)

The 1963 tipper had an 89bhp 5-litre six-cylinder diesel. The 5.8-litre engine was an option but a five-speed gearbox was standard.

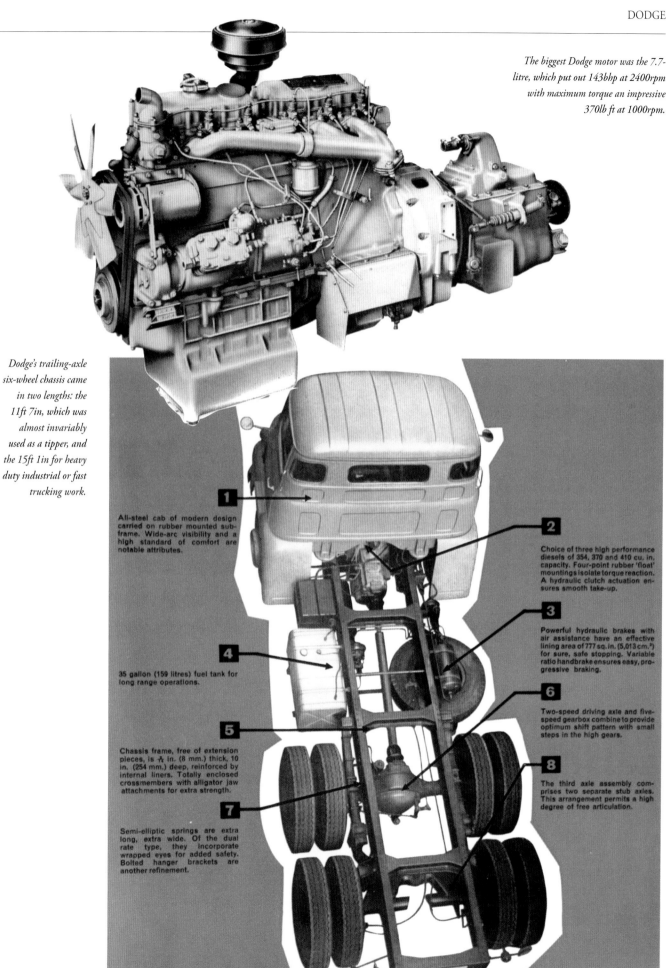

The biggest Dodge motor was the 7.7-litre, which put out 143bhp at 2400rpm with maximum torque an impressive 370lb ft at 1000rpm.

Dodge's trailing-axle six-wheel chassis came in two lengths: the 11ft 7in, which was almost invariably used as a tipper, and the 15ft 1in for heavy duty industrial or fast trucking work.

1
All-steel cab of modern design carried on rubber mounted sub-frame. Wide-arc visibility and a high standard of comfort are notable attributes.

2
Choice of three high performance diesels of 354, 370 and 410 cu. in. capacity. Four-point rubber 'float' mountings isolate torque reaction. A hydraulic clutch actuation ensures smooth take-up.

3
Powerful hydraulic brakes with air assistance have an effective lining area of 777 sq. in. (5,013 cm.²) for sure, safe stopping. Variable ratio handbrake ensures easy, progressive braking.

4
35 gallon (159 litres) fuel tank for long range operations.

6
Two-speed driving axle and five-speed gearbox combine to provide optimum shift pattern with small steps in the high gears.

5
Chassis frame, free of extension pieces, is 5/16 in. (8 mm.) thick, 10 in. (254 mm.) deep, reinforced by internal liners. Totally enclosed crossmembers with alligator jaw attachments for extra strength.

8
The third axle assembly comprises two separate stub axles. This arrangement permits a high degree of free articulation.

7
Semi-elliptic springs are extra long, extra wide. Of the dual rate type, they incorporate wrapped eyes for added safety. Bolted hanger brackets are another refinement.

ERF

The sales literature put out by ERF was seldom decorative, concentrating on giving the potential purchaser the hard facts.

Before making its debut at the 1933 Commercial Motor show was a lorry manufactured by a newly-constituted company, E R Foden and Son. This was the result of Edwin Richard Foden, one of the sons of the founder of the old-established firm of Foden, disagreeing with its reluctance to accept that the days of steam-powered road transport were over. Taking his son and a handful of faithful employees with him, Edwin Foden set up in opposition just a few miles away at Sandbach in Cheshire, and started building Gardner diesel-powered vehicles which evolved into the light-weight OE range and the heavy C ranges. A good number of components were bought in.

Relationships between the two factions cannot have been too strained as, when the fledgling firm outgrew its factory space, the old company was quite ready to sell one of its own works to expand into. Both branches of the Foden family were by this time engaged upon the construction of diesel-powered commercials, but the newer firm was more innovative and in 1937 came up the with the first Chinese Six twin-steering six-wheeler.

ERF production continued during the war years, a good number of heavy four-wheelers from the C range going into army service, some fitted with AEC diesels to augment the supply of Gardners.

Like so many other manufacturers ERF continued with what were essentially its pre-war models immediately after hostilities had ceased, and it was not until 1948 that its products' looks were updated with a mildly modernised cab featuring a curved dummy radiator.

Although technical improvements continued to be made in areas such as the braking system, it was not until 1956 that a fresh look was given to ERF's standard range of trucks with the introduction of the KV cab, which had a wrap-around two-piece windscreen and an oval radiator grill. From then on, where it was considered practicable, Cummings and Rolls-Royce diesel engines were used, although the Gardner still remained the mainstay power plant.

Another cab update was carried out during 1961. The cabs were still supplied by Jennings, who had done so since the firm built its first lorries nearly 30 years before; in fact Jennings was to become part of the company within a short while.

In addition to its conventional products for the road transport industry ERF also manufactured dump trucks, as well as Cummins-powered tractor units for the Middle East with a 50-ton capability. Another diversification was undertaken during the later part of the 1960s when the company started producing fire engines, but in the mid-1970s this activity was abandoned as ERF concentrated on developing of load-carrying commercials that would comply with European standards and the requirements of continental long-distance hauliers.

In 1996 the company was bought by Western Star, a Canadian company, which then sold it to MAN in 2000. Today lorries wearing the ERF badge are manufactured in Germany.

SPECIFICATION OF
MODEL C.I.5.
CAPACITY 7½ TONS
With Trailer 13 Tons

ERF
OIL ENGINED VEHICLES

E.R.F. LTD.
MANAGING DIRECTORS : E. R. FODEN, D. FODEN
SUN WORKS
SANDBACH
CHESHIRE
TELEPHONE 223-4-5 SANDBACH
TELEGRAMS "ERF" SANDBACH

The first postwar brochure for the C1.5, a number of which had been supplied to the RASC during hostilities, featured photographs of vehicles still fitted with wartime blackout masks on the headlamps. As the vehicle was essentially unchanged since the late 1930s this was of little import. A Gardner 5LW engine was used in conjunction with a five-speed gearbox. Servo-assisted hydraulic brakes were fitted to all models, with a quickly detachable vacuum coupling and balancing system on the tractor and semi-trailer.

FITTED WITH
THE FAMOUS
GARDNER
E N G I N E

ERF — OIL ENGINED VEHICLES

LEADING DIMENSIONS	TYPE C.1.5. Standard Wheelbase.	TYPE C.1.5. Tractor.	TYPE C.1.5. Tractor & Semi-Trailer
	ft. in.	ft. in.	ft. in.
Body Length (inside)	16 9	—	22 0
Wheelbase	12 11	8 5	8' 5" & 14' 0"
Length Overall	22 8	13 9	29 3¾
Width ,, ...	7 5	7 5	7 5
Height ,, (unladen)	8 0½	8 0½	8 0½
Track Front at Ground	6 4¼	6 4¼	6 4¼
Track Rear ,, ,, ...	5 4⅝	5 4⅝	5 4⅝
Frame Height, Loaded	2 10	2 10	2 10
Platform Height, Loaded	3 9	—	4 2
Turning Circle	52 0	36 0	41 0
Unladen Weight (with Standard Body and Cab) ..	4 tons 5 cwts.	3 tons 16 cwts.	6 tons 5 cwts.

ROAD SPEEDS	Fifth	Fourth	Third	Second	First	Reverse
Engine Running at 1,700 r.p.m. Back Axle Ratio, 7·25 : 1	34·30 m.p.h.	26·20 m.p.h.	14·50 m.p.h.	7·73 m.p.h.	4·02 m.p.h.	3·97 m.p.h

The 1953 Model 5.6 was available as a tipper with 12ft 9in wheelbase or flatbed lorry with one of 16ft 6in. Engine was a 5LW Gardner five-cylinder diesel of 7 litres producing 85bhp at 1700rpm, and drive to the overhead worm drive rear axles was through a five-speed gearbox.

Wheelbase of the 5.6 TS (Twin Steer) was 17ft 2in, and for some mysterious reason, although it had the same Gardner engine as the 5.6, the ERF brochure credited it with 94bhp. The highest ratio of its five-speed gearbox allowed a maximum road speed at 1700rpm of 31.4mph, and the vehicle had hydraulic servo brakes with a pump driven from the gearbox.

This was the look, distinguished by a range of colour covers, of ERF's sales material, and with few exceptions the frontal aspect of the vehicles themselves was of uniform appearance.

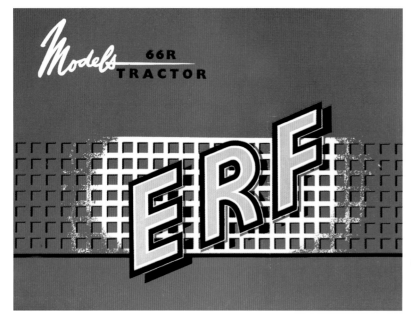

The 66 range of tractors all had the same 12.17-litre Rolls-Royce C6NFR Series 129 six-cylinder diesel engine, which produced 200bhp at 2100rpm. It normally drove through a five-speed constant-mesh gearbox with epicyclic two-speed auxiliary, giving ten speeds in all. Alternatively a torque converter could be fitted to the rear of the motor, driving a three-speed gearbox. There was a range of six different wheelbase lengths, from 12ft to 15ft 9in, and three methods of bogie drive from single or double reduction to hypoid and hub reduction for gross weights of over 50 tons.

A mainly off-road dumper, the 54G of 1958 had an 11ft 9in wheelbase and a capacity of 7 cubic yards. It was powered by a Gardner 5LW motor with five-speed gearbox. For overseas or for operation in abnormal terrain, either a Gardner 6LW (112bhp) or a 6LX (150bhp) could be specified.

54Gs and 56Gs came in four different guises. The tipper had a wheelbase of 12ft 8in and either a 7-litre Gardner 5LW (54G) or an 8.4-litre Gardner 6LW.

Standard truck wheelbase was 15ft 3in, with either 14ft or 16ft 7in available if required. Whether it was a 54G or a 56G depended, as with the tipper, on its motor. In all cases a five-speed gearbox was employed. Brakes were hydraulic with Hydrovac servo assistance.

The rare 66GSF tipper had a 13ft 3in wheelbase and was powered by the Gardner 6LW. It also was made as a truck with wheelbase of either 16ft 1in or 17ft 5in. All had five-speed gearboxes and double-drive axles with overhead worm and wheel and provision for a third differential if required. Their smaller relation, the 56GSF, had a Gardner 5LW motor with all same wheelbase and body configurations but either single-drive with twin-speed axle or double-drive as on the 66. Brakes on all types were hydraulic with air servo assistance.

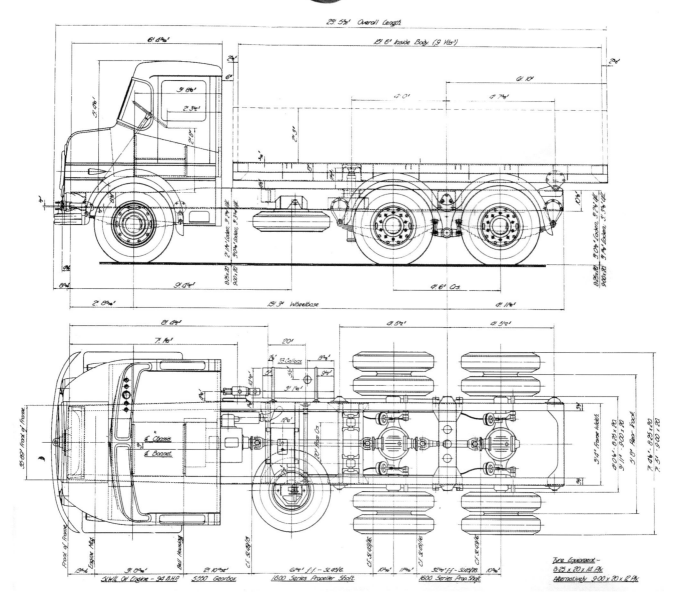

ERF

Model LKG 44

Four Cylinder

Four Wheeler

9 TONS GROSS

6 Tons Payload (Approx.)

A tipper with 8ft 10in wheelbase and two trucks of 11ft 4in and 12ft 10in wheelbase constituted the LKG44 range for 1959. A Gardner 4LK engine was fitted in conjunction with a five-speed gearbox.

The twin-steer ERFs had a choice of three engines, all by Gardner: the 56TSG had a 5LW, the 66TSG a 6LW and the 66TSGX a 6LX. There was a tipper with 14ft wheelbase and two trucks with 17ft 2in and 19ft wheelbase. All had five-speed gearboxes and air assisted brakes

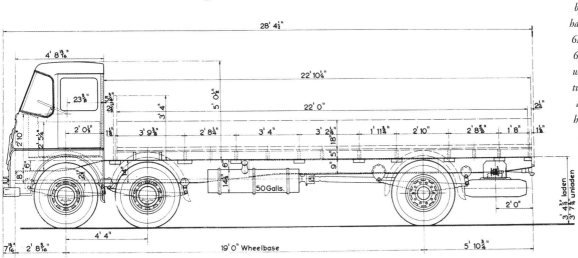

44G tractors had an 8ft 9in wheelbase and Gardner 4LW motor. 54Gs had one of 8ft 6in with a Gardner 5LW. 64Gs had an 8ft 10in with a 6LW and the 64GXs had either a 9ft wheelbase or one of 10ft 1in with the big Gardner 6LX.

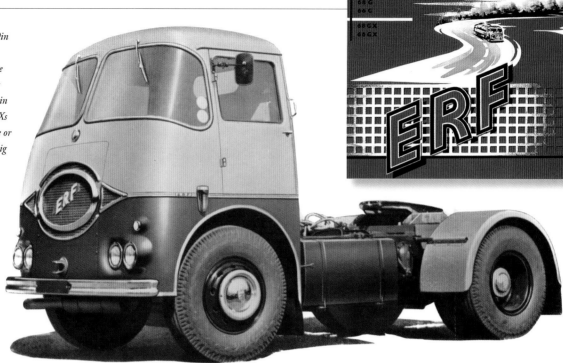

The Gs had the Gardner 6LW motor and the GXs a 6LX. There were four lengths of wheelbase for the tipper: 12ft 6in, 14ft 7in, 15ft 8in and 16ft 7in. The latter also doubled as the shortest one for a truck, which was also available with a 17ft 9in 18ft wheelbase. Five-speed gearboxes and double-drive rear bogies were de rigueur.

During 1960 twin headlights were introduced. This cab is unusual in that it has an integral name panel above the windscreen. One feature of this firm's thoroughly practical designs was towing jaws front and rear, the former prominent below the radiator grille.

The 1961 four-cylinder could carry 9 tons. All ERF cabs were rubber mounted, as were the majority of other commercials and, also in common with others, flashing indicators were optional.

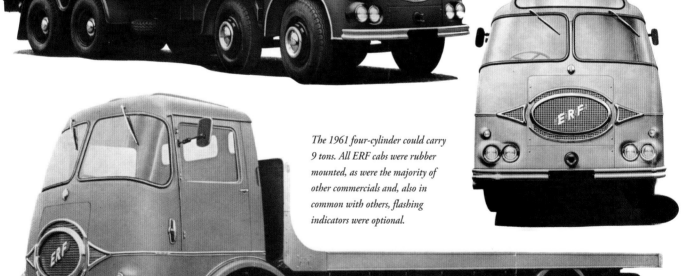

FODEN

The war had just been won and the drive was on to re-establish export orders. Why on earth, for this English language export brochure of 1946, did they call themselves and their products Poden?

Edwin Foden started working life as an apprentice in the 1850s at Plant and Hancock, Agricultural Engineers. Before too many years had passed he rose to become first a partner, and then to take control of the firm that was now named Hancock and Foden. Although this enterprise already manufactured stationary and portable steam engines, Edwin Foden was determined to develop a successful self-propelled vehicle, and by the time of the War Office Trials of 1901 this had come to fruition. The company, now named simply E Foden and Sons, from then on and for the next 30-odd years manufactured exclusively steam-powered commercial vehicles. Until the mid-1920s these ran on solid rubber tyres and were chain-driven, but during 1925 the firm introduced its E type, with shaft drive, and shortly after this the sophisticated Speed Six, with pneumatic tyres, a claimed top speed of around 60mph, and four-wheel steam brakes to rein in the behemoth.

By the early 1930s the age of steam for road vehicles was rapidly passing and Foden began to switch over to diesel power, but this did not happen soon enough for one of Edwin's sons, who abandoned ship and set up in opposition, calling his company E R Foden (ERF). Edwin had died in 1911 and had been succeeded by his two sons Edwin Richard and William, who emigrated to Australia.

To begin with the firm's traditional customers seemed to be shopping elsewhere, and certainly the various classes from 4 to 12 tons were not a great success, only the larger 15-tonner finding favour with the haulage contractors of the mid-1930s. An upturn in sales came about after 1935, when William returned from the Antipodes and oversaw the introduction of the DG series, which proved the firm's saviour. Indeed, by the time war broke out this model was sufficiently proven to be considered suitable to be militarised, and production of it was maintained, alongside the tanks and ordnance that the firm was also called upon to produce.

With the coming of peace the pre-war models were soon updated to become the FG series, and in addition both single- and double-decker buses began to be built. It was shortly after this that Foden was asked to build a sizeable dump truck for a steel firm in South Wales; this proved to be the first of a long line of large dump trucks that became something of a speciality. At around the same time the company started to produce its own diesel engine, a supercharged two-stroke of just over 4 litres.

The 1950s saw the dump truck business go from strength to strength, and there was an addition to the range in the form of heavy tractors, capable of dealing with payloads of up to 80 tons.

In line with many other manufacturers Foden began

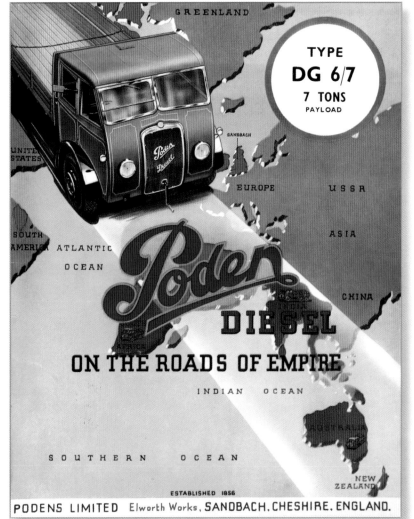

GREENLAND

TYPE
DG 6/7
7 TONS
PAYLOAD

UNITED STATES

SANDBACH

EUROPE

U S S R

SOUTH AMERICA

ATLANTIC OCEAN

ASIA

Poden

DIESEL

CHINA

ON THE ROADS OF EMPIRE

INDIAN OCEAN

AUSTRALIA

SOUTHERN OCEAN

NEW ZEALAND

ESTABLISHED 1856

PODENS LIMITED Elworth Works, SANDBACH, CHESHIRE, ENGLAND.

to use fibreglass for cab construction from the late 1950s and then, in 1962, maintenance-friendly tilting cabs were introduced. The monster Rolls-Royce-powered dumper was also made at this time; its chassis could also be used as a crane platform. The largest dump trucks had a capacity of some 40 tons, but the line was discontinued in the mid-1960s.

Changes in government regulation were cleverly circumnavigated in 1964 with the introduction of the Foden Twin Load, a rigid eight-wheeler to which could be attached to a single-axle semi-trailer allowing the whole to be used up to the 32-ton maximum.

During the 1970s a very large NATO contract for military vehicles went somewhat awry and nearly took the firm under; even the Master tractor units brought out later on in the decade failed to restore its finances. During 1980 the receivers were called in and the company was acquired by the American conglomerate Paccar, under whose aegis it exists to this day, if in name only, production of Fodens having been transferred to Leyland.

The 16ft 1in wheelbase Foden 5/12 with van body could carry 12 tons..

The standard truck wheelbase for the DG 6/7 was 13ft 7½in but a tractor unit with one of 8ft ¾in and a tipper of 11ft were also made. A Gardner 6LW was used in conjunction with a Foden four-speed gearbox and Foden overhead worm drive rear axle.

The Foden 6/15 standard truck would cope with 15 tons and had a 13ft 7½in wheelbase.

This could be either a FG5/12 with Gardner 5LW motor or a FG6/12 with Gardner 6LW; either way the wheelbase was 16ft 1in.

The Foden four-spring bogie with swing link. Axles were interchangeable.

A unique feature was the mounting of the speedometer along with horn and panel light switches in the centre of the steering wheel. Lighting switches, ammeter and fuses were all contained in the scuttle-mounted box.

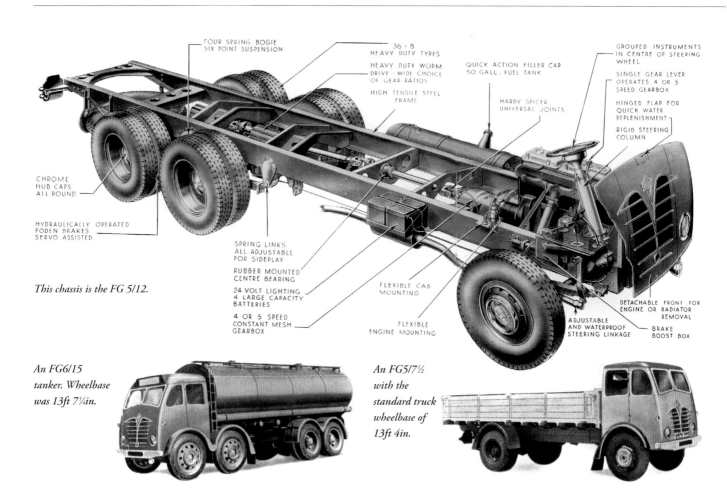

FOUR SPRING BOGIE
SIX POINT SUSPENSION

36 × 8
HEAVY DUTY TYRES

QUICK ACTION FILLER CAP
50 GALL. FUEL TANK

GROUPED INSTRUMENTS
IN CENTRE OF STEERING
WHEEL

HEAVY DUTY WORM
DRIVE - WIDE CHOICE
OF GEAR RATIOS

SINGLE GEAR LEVER
OPERATES 4 OR 5
SPEED GEARBOX

HIGH TENSILE STEEL
FRAME

HARDY SPICER
UNIVERSAL JOINTS

HINGED FLAP FOR
QUICK WATER
REPLENISHMENT

RIGID STEERING
COLUMN

CHROME
HUB CAPS
ALL ROUND

HYDRAULICALLY OPERATED
FODEN BRAKES
SERVO ASSISTED

SPRING LINKS
ALL ADJUSTABLE
FOR SIDEPLAY

RUBBER MOUNTED
CENTRE BEARING

FLEXIBLE CAB
MOUNTING

24 VOLT LIGHTING
4 LARGE CAPACITY
BATTERIES

FLEXIBLE
ENGINE MOUNTING

4 OR 5 SPEED
CONSTANT MESH
GEARBOX

ADJUSTABLE
AND WATERPROOF
STEERING LINKAGE

DETACHABLE FRONT FOR
ENGINE OR RADIATOR
REMOVAL

BRAKE
BOOST BOX

This chassis is the FG 5/12.

An FG6/15 tanker. Wheelbase was 13ft 7¼in.

An FG5/7½ with the standard truck wheelbase of 13ft 4in.

Although the company's brochure covers were generally uninspired in the later 1950s their notepaper was a delight.

ROAD TRANSPORT *Foden* VEHICLE MANUFACTURERS

FODENS LIMITED

BY APPOINTMENT
TO THE LATE KING GEORGE V

Directors
J WILD
W FODEN

Telegrams
"FODENWAY"

Visibility was excellent from the updated cabs but the multipiece screens gave an old-fashioned look.

The four-wheeler's capacity was 14 tons gross load but the big eight-wheeler pick ups could manage 24 tons.

Dump Truck. 56,000 lbs. payload, 300 b.h.p. engine, torque converter.

Foden, in addition to their regular range, had made a speciality of bespoke commercials for a myriad of different purposes. They had also developed a selection of businesslike dumper trucks for industries such as mining and construction which enjoyed a worldwide market. This is one of their larger ones.

By 1964 cabs were manufactured of glassfibre and could be tilted for maintenance. Standard eight-wheelers had a 13ft 7¼in wheelbase and were rated at 24 tons gross. A five-speed gearbox was normal but one with seven speeds was an option.

STANDARD SIX CYLINDER
175 B.H.P. ENGINE

The four-wheeler's wheelbase could be 12ft 3in, 14ft 3in or 16ft 1in. Bendix-Westinghouse air brakes were employed on all Foden trucks.

Foden had been manufacturing their own engines for a good while and these were normally fitted although either a Gardner 5LW or 6LW could still be specified by the customer. Four-wheelers and twin-steer six-wheelers used the 3.2-litre four-cylinder FD 4 whilst the 20-ton six-wheelers and 24-ton eight-wheelers used the 4.8-litre six-cylinder FD6. An uprated turbocharged version of the latter, giving 225bhp, was an option for the 24-tonners.

There were three wheelbase options for the eight-wheeler in addition to the standard truck: 9ft 9½in, 11ft ¼in and 11ft 10in.

FORD

For their first postwar commercials Ford stuck with rod-operated brakes.

Before moving to Dagenham in Essex during 1931 the Ford Motor Company had built trucks for the UK market, very similar to its American products, at Trafford Park in Manchester, as well as Fordson road tractors at its factory in Southern Ireland. The first trucks manufactured at the new purpose-built Thameside factory were badged Ford and had a capacity of 1-ton but, from 1933, all vehicles in the commercial range were given the title Fordson. The first of these were forward-control 2-tonners.

Within the next two years further models up to 3 tons were added, and around the same time the company's famous V8 sidevalve motor, which had for some time been used in Ford cars, began to be used in the commercials.

By 1939 the range had been enlarged still further to include a forward-control 5-tonner and, shortly after, there was another name change, Fordson Thames from now on being the brand name of all English Ford commercials.

Once the United States became embroiled in the Second World War, Ford's manufacturing contribution was enormous: Liberator bombers as well as that enduring icon, the Jeep, are just two examples of its US wartime output. Ford in Britain, although obviously a much smaller operation, threw its entire weight behind the war effort from the outset. Some 200,000 military vehicles, from trucks to Bren gun carriers, and over 250,000 V8 engines, destined for all manner of applications, were turned out by the Essex workforce. In addition, a satellite factory in the Manchester area was set up, producing some 30,000

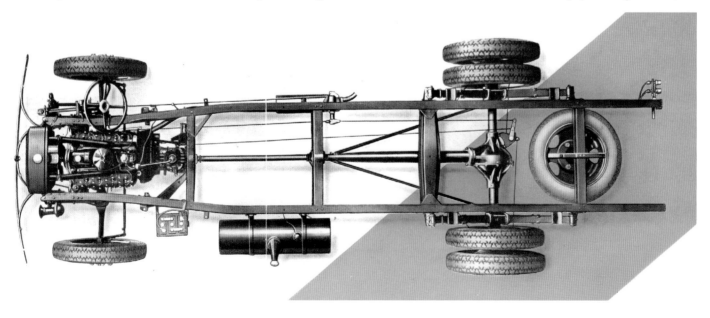

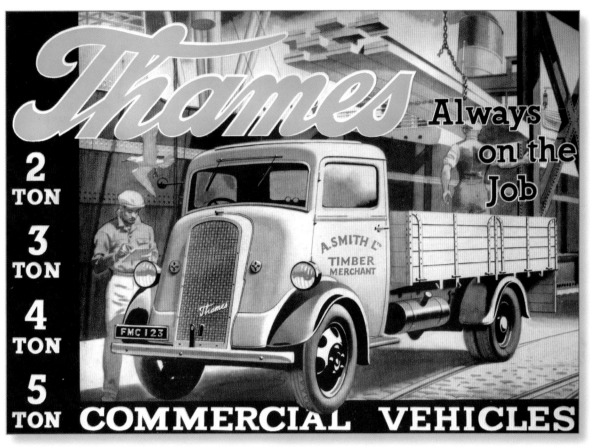

Rolls-Royce Merlin aero engines.

With the war won, the ubiquitous V8 motor continued to be used in the forward-control 2- to 5-tonners which made up the initial postwar output. These were replaced, by 1950, with a new bonneted range of petrol and diesel lorries, the largest of which could carry 8 tons. Somewhat surprisingly, as Ford was an early advocate of self sufficiency, it was not until 1954 that it began to produce its own diesel engine, a four-cylinder of just over 3½ litres which began to be offered as an alternative to the petrol version from which it had been developed.

In 1957, coinciding with the introduction of the new Trader trucks, Ford renamed its commercial vehicle arm once again. For the next few years they were branded as Ford Thames. The Thames Traders, as they became known, could be had from launch with either petrol or diesel engines and from 30cwt to 7-ton capacity, with other specialist versions being added as time went by. The early 1960s saw further developments to the range including a bonneted version, and options were offered such as five-speed gearboxes and two-speed axles in an attempt to keep a successful but increasingly dated design youthful. A new generation of commercials was in the pipeline and, as if to signify this new age and at the same time unify its interna-

THAMES 2 TON FULLY ENCLOSED VAN
ON 118 in. WHEELBASE CHASSIS

If built as a tractor unit, the 9ft 10in chassis had a lower rear axle ratio and was able to handle a payload of 8 tons.

THAMES CHASSIS AND CAB, WITH BRITISH TRAILER
FOUR-IN-LINE ARTICULATED TRAILER

By 1950 the new Thames range comprised: an articulated tractor unit and a 4 cubic yard tipper with 10ft 2 in wheelbase; 2-, 3-, 4-, and 5-ton trucks and the Sussex six-wheeler chassis with 10ft 8in wheelbase; and 4- and 5-tonners and Sussex six-wheeler with 13ft 1in wheelbase. The 3-, 4- and 5-tonners were available with a Perkins P6 diesel engine as an alternative to the Ford V8 if required. Brakes were now hydraulic and anything larger than the 2-tonner had vacuum servo assistance.

Ford's sidevalve V8 had first seen the light of day in the early 1930s and since then, as well as its makers' intended applications, had been used by other car manufacturers for their own products. It had also been a favourite power unit with special builders on both sides of the Atlantic, often being persuaded to produce power far beyond Henry Ford's original intention. Tens of thousands powered military vehicles in World War II.

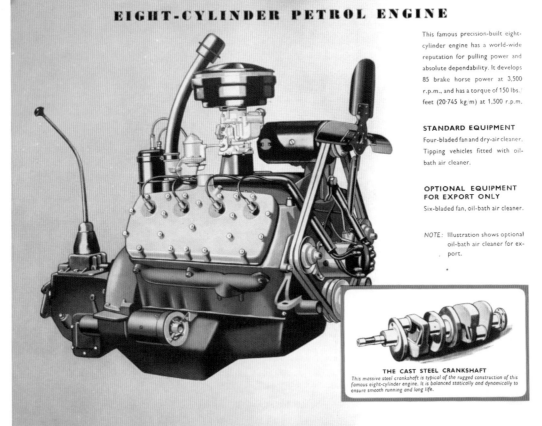

EIGHT-CYLINDER PETROL ENGINE

This famous precision-built eight-cylinder engine has a world-wide reputation for pulling power and absolute dependability. It develops 85 brake horse power at 3,500 r.p.m., and has a torque of 150 lbs./ feet (20·745 kg/m) at 1,500 r.p.m.

STANDARD EQUIPMENT
Four-bladed fan and dry-air cleaner. Tipping vehicles fitted with oil-bath air cleaner.

OPTIONAL EQUIPMENT FOR EXPORT ONLY
Six-bladed fan, oil-bath air cleaner.

NOTE: Illustration shows optional oil-bath air cleaner for export.

THE CAST STEEL CRANKSHAFT
This massive steel crankshaft is typical of the rugged construction of this famous eight-cylinder engine. It is balanced statically and dynamically to ensure smooth running and long life.

tional image, during 1965 the company reverted to the name that they had used on their very first British-manufactured trucks – Ford.

Of Ford's new generation the Transit in all its forms has endured, albeit unrecognisable from its early embodiment, through four decades. Its success resulted from the almost magical way it demonstrated to a whole generation that a light commercial could go, handle and have street credibility comparable with the majority of private cars, while also fulfilling a multiplicity of roles from workhorse to out-of-hours passion wagon.

The second of the new generation was the D series of tilt-cab trucks, the majority of which were diesel-powered though there was a petrol option. Initially they ranged from 2 to 9 tons capacity. By the end of the 1960s this family had grown to encompass rigid trucks up to 24 tons and tractors up to 28 tons, these largest of the series being powered by V8 diesels.

The end for the D series came in 1981, when it was replaced by the forward-looking Cargo range, and from that time onwards Ford has continued to build upon the position which it first attained in 1977, that of Britain's foremost manufacturer of commercial vehicles.

The Big 'THAMES' Chassis*

Gear Box
Four-speed heavy-duty gear box with provision for power take off

Fully-floating rear axle with full range of optional axle ratio's

Heavy chrome alloy steel springs. Material tensile strength 200,000 per sq. in.

Heavily ribbed differential housing minimizes axle distortion under heavy loads

Self-energizing hydraulic brakes, Servo assistance on models over 2 tons

'THAMES' Chassis are available with left-hand or right-hand drive. (Radiator grill shown for illustration purposes only).

Shock Absorbers
Double-acting hydraulic shock absorbers

Front Axle
Drop forged 'I' section beam. Material tensile strength 150,000 lb. per sq. in.

Ford encouraged manufacturers of bespoke commercials to use their chassis, and the preferred companies had their products promoted alongside Dagenham's own in the more comprehensive brochures, such as this one from 1950.

'THAMES' TRACTOR UNITS

for Articulated Vehicles and for General Trailer Work

The Thames extra short wheelbase (122 in. – 3·10 metres) Chassis and Cab can be adapted for use with semi Trailers or full Trailers made by the British Trailer Company Limited, Carrimore Six Wheelers Limited, and other well-known manufacturers.

This sturdy tractor unit, with heavy-duty chassis frame and 34 × 7 tyres all round, gives a maximum permissible laden weight of 260 cwts. when coupled with a semi Trailer also fitted with 34 × 7 tyres.

The combination of Thames chassis cab with semi Trailer equipment provides the ideal vehicle for the operator who requires extra load carrying capacity for the lowest possible cost.

HEAVY-DUTY PICK-UP
(EXPORT ONLY)

This vehicle is based on the 'Thames' 2-ton (2032 kg.), 128 in. (3·25 m.) wheelbase chassis with windshield supplied with two front doors. The cab is fitted with a full width special bench-type seat accommodating two passengers in addition to the driver. The all-steel cab roof is double skinned and fully insulated with Isoflex. It is extended towards the rear of the vehicle, giving protection to the three passengers who can be accommodated on another special bench-type seat fitted behind the partition.

The body is of all-steel construction and the tailboard and sides are double panelled. ⅛ in. (·32 cm.) steel plate is used on the floor which is substantially supported by steel channel sections, runners and bearers.

OVERALL DIMENSIONS

Length	18 ft. 0 in. (4·57 m.)
Width	7 ft. 0 in. (2·134 m.)
Height	7 ft. 6 in. (2·286 m.)
Unladen Weight	5740 lbs. (2603 kg.)

The JEKTA

5-Ton (5082 kilos) Telescopic Ejector General Purpose Vehicle

The body of this vehicle consists of three 'U' shaped scuppers arranged to telescope into each other for the purpose of expelling the load. The movement of the scuppers on the running rails is obtained by a patented design of double-acting hydraulic ram. Some of the many advantages of this revolutionary type body are: stresses and strains imposed by normal tipping bodies are eliminated, thus prolonging chassis life—stabilizing effect of horizontal discharge—economy of manpower when only partial discharge is required and the ability to discharge in low headroom.

OVERALL DIMENSIONS

Length	20 ft. 11·75 in. (6·40 m.)
Width	6 ft. 11 in. (2·11 m.)
Height	7 ft. 5·5 in. (2·27 m.)
Unladen Weight	7161 lbs. (3248 kg.)
Body Capacity	6 cu. yds. (4·59 cu. m.)

DE LUXE (*Facing Forward*)
THREE-HORSE BOX

This 'De Luxe' Horse Box body by Lambourn Garages Ltd. affords the greatest possible comfort to both horses and men. It accommodates three horses all facing forward. Movable bucket seats are provided for four grooms in the driver's compartment so that grooms and driver are in direct contact with the horses at all times. The stalls are fully padded throughout and a detachable manger is provided for each horse. The loading ramps are fitted with a patent controller which makes opening and closing easy and eliminates bounce when the ramp is lowered. The body is specially constructed to give the lowest possible loading height. There are two spacious baggage compartments at the back—one on either side of the rear stall.

Mounted on the 'Thames' 4-ton (4,000 kg.) chassis and powered by the famous eight-cylinder 'Thames' engine, this vehicle provides the finest and safest form of transport for valuable, highly-trained horses. It is specially suitable for long journeys.

OVERALL DIMENSIONS

Length	25 ft. 6 in. (7·77 m.)
Width	7 ft. 6 in. (2·29 m.)
Height	10 ft. 6 in. (3·20 m.)
Unladen Weight	3 ton 18 cwt. 2 qrs. (8,792 lbs.) (3,987 kgs.)

THAMES
COMMERCIAL VEHICLES

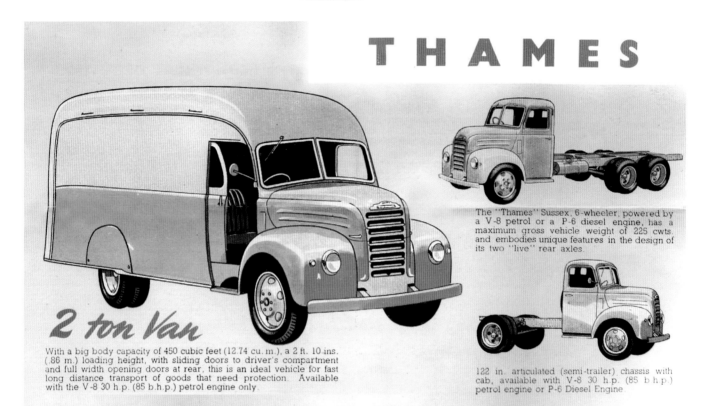

THAMES

THAMES

2 ton Van

With a big body capacity of 450 cubic feet (12.74 cu. m.), a 2 ft. 10 ins. (.86 m.) loading height, with sliding doors to driver's compartment and full width opening doors at rear, this is an ideal vehicle for fast long distance transport of goods that need protection. Available with the V-8 30 h.p. (85 b.h.p.) petrol engine only.

The "Thames" Sussex, 6-wheeler, powered by a V-8 petrol or a P-6 diesel engine, has a maximum gross vehicle weight of 225 cwts. and embodies unique features in the design of its two "live" rear axles.

122 in. articulated (semi-trailer) chassis with cab, available with V-8 30 h.p. (85 b.h.p.) petrol engine or P-6 Diesel Engine.

THAMES

The first years of the 1950s saw the standard range continuing virtually unaltered.

- ◆ "Thames" semi-forward control commercial vehicles from 2 to 8 tons.
- ◆ 128 in. and 157 in. wheelbases for truck operation.
- ◆ 122 in. wheelbase for tipper (Dump Truck) operation, and semi-trailer use.
- ◆ V-8 30 h.p. (85 b.h.p.) engine available on all models.
- ◆ P-6 diesel 6-cylinder engine available on all models except 2-ton vehicles.
- ◆ All models supplied with complete cab, or with cab front end only, according to your requirements.
- ◆ A range of standard bodies and of special bodies for Municipal and other particular uses.

Although this catalogue is dated 1955 it remained current for several more years. The 30cwt model had the same wheelbase, at 10ft 2in, as the shortest of its larger relations. The entire 30cwt to 4-ton range was available in three versions other than a complete vehicle so that a wide variety of special bodies could be built for them.

CHASSIS WITH CAB

POWERFUL—RELIABLE—ECONOMICAL

CHASSIS WITH WINDSCREEN

CHASSIS WITH CAB FITTINGS

THAMES 30 CWT. MODELS

- Full width, all-steel cab, robustly constructed, fully reinforced and flexibly mounted on six special rubber cushions.
- Rugged chassis frame of suitable design for the mounting of all types of special bodies.
- Four-cylinder O.H.V. petrol or diesel engine, incorporating all desirable modern design features to ensure high performance, lasting satisfaction and maximum economy.
- Four-speed heavy duty gearbox with well selected gear ratios.
- Worm and roller type steering giving easy action and complete control under all road conditions.
  - Double acting hydraulic shock absorbers on the front axle, providing smooth riding and extra load protection.
  - Fully floating rear axle with 5.14 : 1 ratio.
  - Hydraulically operated self-energising brakes with 14 in. diameter drums giving a total brake lining area of 273.6 sq. ins.
  - 12-volt electrical system.

VAN MODELS

Your Ford Dealer will be glad to supply all relevant information in connection with van bodies and to quote you for types which may be built to meet your special requirements.

In 1953 Ford had brought out an entirely new ohv four-cylinder 100 x 115mm 3.6-litre petrol engine, giving 70bhp, for their commercials. This was joined a year later by a 60bhp diesel version of identical capacity and dimensions, and either one or other of these engines was, according to customer's preference, now used in all Ford commercials up to 4-tonners.

DIESEL ENGINE SPECIFICATION

ENGINE
Four-cylinder. Direct injection. Bore 3.94" (100 mm.). Stroke 4.52" (115 mm.). Capacity 220 cu. ins. (3.6 litres). Max. B.H.P. 60 at 2,400 r.p.m. (governed). Max. Torque 150-lb. ft. at 1,600 r.p.m. Compression ratio 16 : 1. Firing order 1, 2, 4, 3. Detachable cast iron cylinder head. Replaceable wet cylinder liners. Crankshaft with induction hardened main and pin journals. Five main bearings, 3" dia. (76.25 mm.). Aluminium alloy pistons, with three compression and two oil control rings. Fully floating gudgeon pins 1.25" dia. (31 mm.). Engine suspension at three points on rubber. Hydraulic engine stabiliser.

LUBRICATION
Oil pump, self priming, delivering under pressure to main bearings, connecting rod and camshaft bearings. Full flow cartridge type filter. Capacity of sump, including filter, 1.75 gallons.

COOLING SYSTEM
Thermo-siphon assisted by centrifugal belt-driven pump. The system incorporates a thermostat. Two-bladed fan. Capacity of system, 3¼ gallons.

FUEL SYSTEM
The fuel is drawn through a removable glass sediment bowl filter by the fuel lift pump and passed through a replaceable cartridge type filter to the injection pump. These filters ensure that no foreign matter enters the injection system. The injection pump meters the fuel oil under pressure to each injector. Leak fuel from the injectors is returned to the 14 gallon capacity main tank.

INJECTION SYSTEM
Injector pump with pneumatic governor and cold starting device. Four-hole injectors.

new THAMES TRADERS 30 cwt. 2 & 3 Tonners

1957 saw the announcement of Ford's uniquely styled new commercial range. It didn't offer any ground-breaking technology but in normal Ford fashion was made of the very best materials and in the main was well thought out. At first a common wheelbase of 9ft 10in sufficed for all except the 3-tonner, which had one of 11ft 6in. The diesel engine had been breathed upon to give another 100rpm, which spelt 64bhp at 2500rpm, but the petrol engine had had its stroke reduced to 95mm making it now 3211cc, with power down to 68bhp.

Winners for Operators

" When you have studied the design and specifications of these entirely new Thames 30 cwt., 2 and 3 Ton Traders you will be more than impressed by the many far-sighted technical developments designed to cut down operating costs.

" I have never seen a range of trucks with such immense possibilities for every large and small operator.

" Let's take a closer look at several new and outstanding Thames 5-Star Trader developments. . . . . . ''

Entirely New Style

" There's no mistaking the new, distinctive Thames Trader style. It's got a new, sturdy character. This new Ford forward control allows a shorter tougher chassis, larger load space, the best balanced weight distribution, and a smaller turning circle.

" Drivers are going to enjoy a new standard of comfort. Operators are going to find their transportation more economical.

" These are important developments in forward control no operator can afford to miss.''

The Improved 4D Diesel Engine

" There's very little I can add to the outstanding reputation of the Ford-made ' 4D ' Diesel. My own operating experience and that of thousands of other operators proves that it is way ahead for performance, low operating costs and reliability. Further developments improve performance and economy.

" The 4 cylinder Ford-made petrol engine is also available.

" These proved power units and the completely new Thames Trader trucks are, without a doubt, the outstanding combination for raising efficiency and increasing all-round economies in every kind of transport work.''

Entirely New Transmission

" The completely new synchromesh gearbox, is designed to do full justice to the brilliant ' 4D ' Diesel and 4 cylinder petrol engines.

" Take a closer look at the new open drive-shaft and extra strong rear axle.

" What I welcome too is the accessibility of the gearbox and differential.

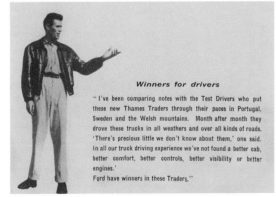

Winners for drivers

" I've been comparing notes with the Test Drivers who put these new Thames Traders through their paces in Portugal, Sweden and the Welsh mountains. Month after month they drove these trucks in all weathers and over all kinds of roads. 'There's precious little we don't know about them,' one said. In all our truck driving experience we've not found a better cab, better comfort, better controls, better visibility or better engines.'

Ford have winners in these Traders,''

Winners for Mechanics

" These new Thames Traders have got all the features I've been wanting for years. They've got the best maintenance accessibility of any forward control truck. Now I've got a truck that will help me to work at greater efficiency. I can carry out routine service or major overhauls with greater speed and ease than ever before. Well done Ford for making my job a lot easier ! ''

'I'm going to drive in style...'

SAYS THE DRIVER

" The economics and engineering of these new Thames Traders, I'll leave to the Guv'nor. But when it comes to cab layout, visibility, and driving, I know what is best suited to my job."

" These new Thames Forward Control Traders are the finest jobs I've yet seen. They're winners !

" Drivers are no longer the forgotten men in truck design. These new cabs improve our working conditions enormously—and that means more efficiency.

" Put yourself in my position—in the driving seat. Comfy isn't it ? There's a shaped metal basepan with a sponge rubber seat—no 'rock-and-roll' for me on the job ! Adjust the seat and see how easily you sit at the controls. Look through the windscreen—it's the largest single-piece screen in any truck. And you can clearly see why we drivers are so particular about it's position. In this cab we can relax and see perfectly. The peep wide screen is near vertical with narrow side pillars. " Visibility couldn't be better.

" Now put your hands on the steering wheel. See the size and angle ? They're dead right. And that neat arm on the right carries the horn button and light switch.

" You can't miss the instrument binnacle. It's just the job : dials, figures and warning lights are large and clear to give us all the facts at a glance.

" Handbrake and gearchange lever are on the left of the driver's seat.

" The cab is a winner ! But I'm equally impressed by the shorter length of the Forward Control chassis, smaller turning circle, and the balanced weight distribution. These are very definite Thames Trader improvements to shorten journeys and speed-up our turn-round.

" Well done Ford ! "

In this very first Trader brochure Ford's advertising department went a little over the top with their superlatives and their desire to extol the modernity of the product - some of this was destined to be edited out of all future editions.

The 'hip' talk of the driver, at least in retrospect, especially when he describes his 'rock and roll' activities, contains unintentional little masterpieces of double entendre.

It must have also been pointed out that the Trader's windscreen was not the largest in the business as this was later watered down to 'one of the biggest single-piece screens in a truck'.

All that aside, including other anomalies such as blue seats captioned as red (again later remedied), the Trader's sales material and the vehicle itself were a breath of fresh air.

Brighter, more comfortable seats

A driver and single passenger seat are standard equipment. A double passenger seat can be obtained as an optional extra. Pressed metal basepans, deep-type foam rubber seats and check-patterned PVC upholstery with red trim provide day-long comfort and brighten up the interior.

Instruments

1. Speedometer Odometer incorporating oil, main beam and generator warning lights. Two panel illumination lights ; fuel gauge, water temperature gauge.
2 (a). Combined ignition key starter-switch—petrol engines.
2 (b). Safety start switch with two positions key operated—Diesel engines.
3. Gear shift indicator diagram (Diesel 3 Ton Trader only).
4. Vacuum gauge (Diesel 3 Ton Trader only).
Thames 3 Ton Diesel Trader Instruments illustrated.

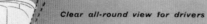

Largest single-piece windscreen

The one piece curved windscreen is made from ¼" toughened glass. The rake is 12½° from the vertical. Dimensions are 16¼ × 63" giving the largest total single piece area of 1,010 sq. ins. There is no centre pillar. The carefully calculated position of the Driver's seat, the large, deep windscreen and the great technical advances achieved by the new Thames Trader Forward Control design provide a high standard of visibility.

Clear all-round view for drivers

In plan view the position of the driver's seat and wide arc of visibility are clearly seen. Much research was carried out to determine the best field of vision for drivers in this new cab. The 5° curve in the wind-screen and the narrow side pillars widen the driver's horizon.

The large full-drop side windows are a Thames Trader feature. They are operated by a winder mechanism.

Complete engine insulation

Research and tests by Ford engineers in a Swedish winter and in tropical temperatures of over 100° F. have developed and proved the engine cab insulation. The engine cowling in the cab is double-skinned with a fibreglass interlining. Cool air is drawn in through the bonnet to form a protective bolster between engine and cab. Engine cooling air is drawn in through the radiator and expelled under the cab floor.

Cool in Summer, Warm in Winter

Owing to the high standard of cab insulation adequate ventilation has been supplied for summer driving. Dual forward vents in the side bulk heads and full drop windows allow a steady even circulation of cool air. For winter driving, space is provided for the easy installation of a dual or single heater unit available as a factory fitted optional extra. The cab is designed to provide every driver with the best working conditions.

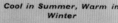

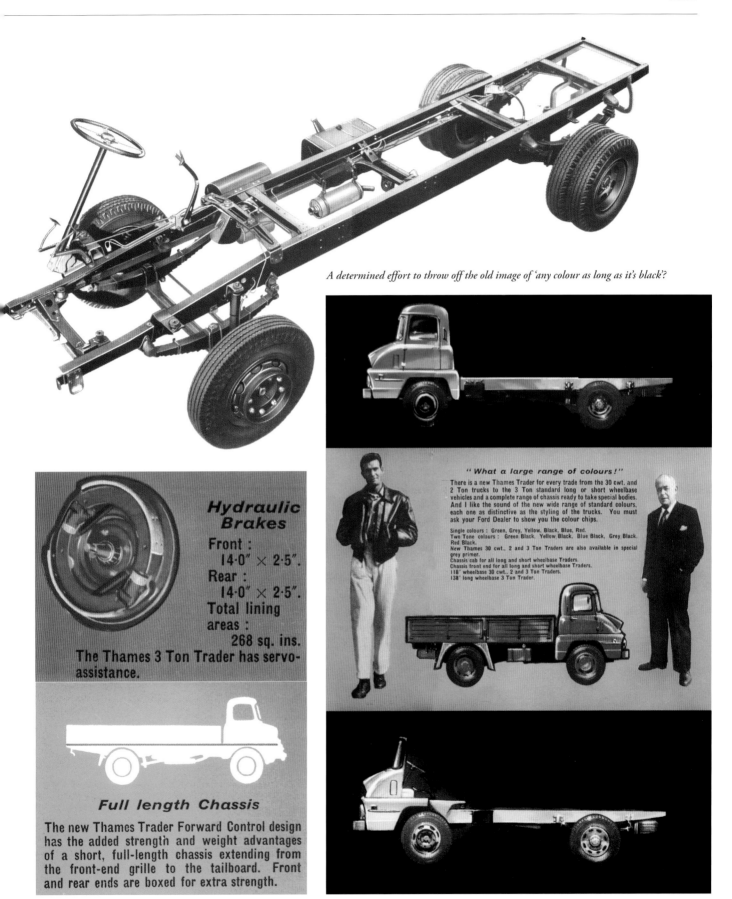

A determined effort to throw off the old image of 'any colour as long as it's black'?

Hydraulic Brakes

Front :
14·0″ × 2·5″.
Rear :
14·0″ × 2·5″.
Total lining
areas :
268 sq. ins.
The Thames 3 Ton Trader has servo-assistance.

Full length Chassis

The new Thames Trader Forward Control design has the added strength and weight advantages of a short, full-length chassis extending from the front-end grille to the tailboard. Front and rear ends are boxed for extra strength.

" What a large range of colours ! "

There is a new Thames Trader for every trade from the 30 cwt. and 2 Ton trucks to the 3 Ton standard long or short wheelbase vehicles and a complete range of chassis ready to take special bodies. And I like the sound of the new wide range of standard colours, each one as distinctive as the styling of the trucks. You must ask your Ford Dealer to show you the colour chips.

Single colours : Green, Grey, Yellow, Black, Blue, Red.
Two Tone colours : Green Black, Yellow Black, Blue Black, Grey Black, Red Black.
New Thames 30 cwt., 2 and 3 Ton Traders are also available in special grey primer.
Chassis cab for all long and short wheelbase Traders.
Chassis front end for all long and short wheelbase Traders.
118″ wheelbase 30 cwt., 2 and 3 Ton Traders.
138″ long wheelbase 3 Ton Trader.

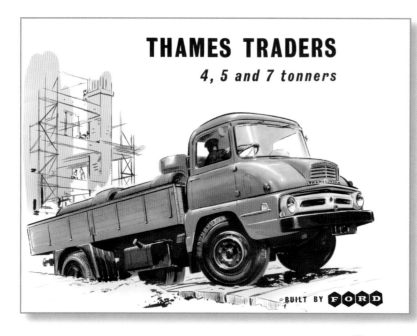

A low-frame version was introduced which ranged from 30cwt to 5 tons, all using the four-cylinder engines and with the same wheelbase dimensions as their standard counterpart.

The larger Traders had six-cylinder versions of the Ford petrol and diesel engines. Thus the diesel, illustrated here, had a capacity of 5416cc with 100bhp at 2500rpm, and the petrol was 4888cc with 114bhp at 3000rpm. The 4- and 5-tonners (11ft 6in or 12ft 10in wheelbase), except tippers (9ft wheelbase), could have four-cylinder engines if desired. The 7-ton truck had either an 11ft 6in or a 13ft 4in wheelbase.

These were constructed on a normal 9ft chassis, reduced to 7ft 9in. The six-cylinder petrol and diesel engines were an option, and in common with all other Traders a four-speed box and single-speed axle were deemed sufficient as standard, although a two-speed axle was available.

THAMES TRADER

ARTICULATED TRACTOR UNIT

with

TASKERS 'D-S' AUTOMATIC COUPLING CONVERSION

THAMES
TRADER
NC
RANGE

TONS 1½·7

The NC series replaced the previous long-running bonneted commercials and its chassis design and other mechanical components were, understandably, very similar or in some cases identical to the Mk II Trader's. Wheelbase dimensions did differ considerably, however: the 30cwt and 2-ton trucks shared one of 11ft; 12ft 2in could accommodate 2-, 3-, 4- or 5-tonners; 13ft 10in did for 3-, 4- or 5-tonners whilst the latter as well as 7-tonners could have longer ones of either 14ft 2in or 15ft 4in. Four-cylinder engines, either petrol or diesel, were standard up to 4 tons, the 5-tonner had either four or six cylinders, while the 7-tonner was a six-cylinder and had a five-speed gearbox as an option. Two-speed axles could be fitted, again as an extra, to any model from 3 tons upwards.

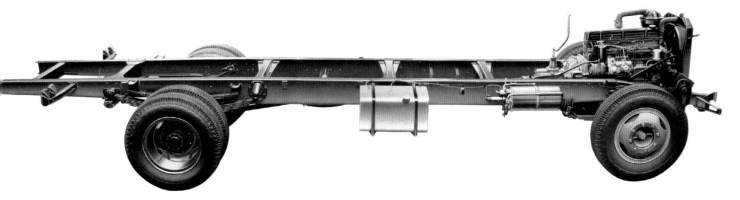

Ford was still keen to offer a variety of special bodies by approved makers, and customers were invited to discuss these with their dealer.

The Mk II Trader had minimal restyling, mostly confined to the repositioning of its name, despite the 'new look' cab spoken of. Quoted engine power, in common with the NC, was up for the four-cylinder engines, the diesel now giving 70bhp and the petrol 73bhp. The petrol six-cylinder's output had gone down to 112bhp but the diesel's had risen to 108bhp – all still with the same capacity. All wheelbase dimensions remained the same as for the previous Traders.

NEW TRADER FC RANGE MK II FROM FORD!

Ford take great pleasure in announcing a new range of Thames Trader forward control trucks. With the typical sturdy Trader look, and the same variety of payloads, 1½ to 10 tons, it has numerous refinements for cutting operating costs to an all time low.

Consider these new features—
* Minimec fuel injection pump on diesel engines for mechanically governed power and reliability.
* Refined and developed 4-speed gearbox for greater durability.
* Optional synchromesh 5-speed gearbox on 6-cylinder models from 5 tons for greater flexibility.
* Brand new heavy duty rear axle, now rated at 18,500 lbs, for 7- and 7½-tonners, 6 cu. yd. tippers.
* Quality improvements to the engines for maximum reliability and increased engine life.
* The "new look" 3-man cab gives excellent driver comfort, and the new extra large exterior mirrors give improved rear visibility.

And there are a host of other detail refinements. Re-engineered throughout and thoroughly tested on road, track, and in thousands of miles of actual operating conditions, the new Trader Mk II FC range is the latest brilliant expression of Ford's unique truck-designing experience.

TRADER FC TRUCKS COST LESS TO OPERATE

The 7½-tonner was the largest in the range apart from the 12-ton (gross) tanker chassis. Six cylinders and a four-speed box were standard but five-speeds or a two-speed axle were extra options.

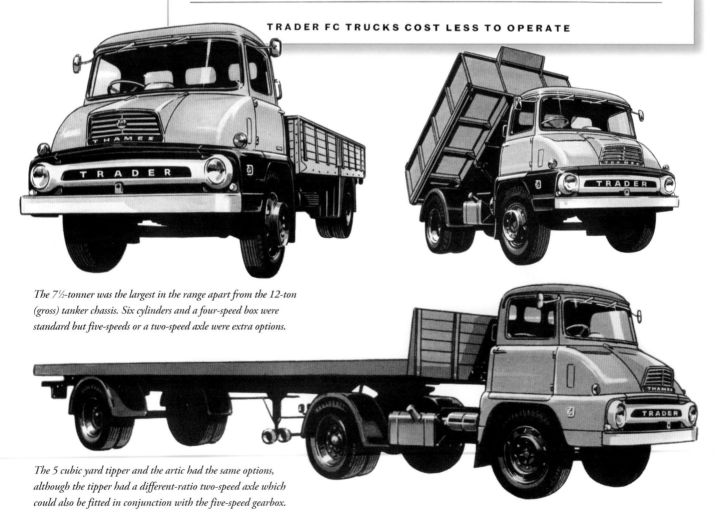

The 5 cubic yard tipper and the artic had the same options, although the tipper had a different-ratio two-speed axle which could also be fitted in conjunction with the five-speed gearbox.

GUY

One might imagine considerably more rakish vehicles to be promoted within the splendid cover of this brochure from the late 1940s.

Only the short-wheelbase chassis had a single propshaft; the two others had a split shaft as here. The engine was a 3686cc four-cylinder petrol unit with a bore and stroke of 95 by 130mm and a torque figure of 165lb ft at 1400rpm of which the manufacturers were rather proud.

Founded just before the outbreak of the First World War by Sydney Slater, previously works manager for the Sunbeam Motor Company, Guy Motors commenced manufacture with just one model. This was a 30cwt commercial with a lightweight pressed steel chassis into which was fitted, on a subframe, a 14.9hp sidevalve petrol engine manufactured by White and Poppe, also the supplier of engines to William Morris for his first venture into car manufacture.

With the onset of war the new factory's efforts were partially turned over to government work. Fortunately, their lorries proved able to withstand the rigours of military use and thus remained in production for a good part of the conflict.

After the war the market was awash with government surplus commercials, but there was still room for good-quality new vehicles and Guy moved into the 1920s with a fresh 2½-ton model. As the decade progressed the firm, in addition to its lorries and passenger vehicles, dabbled with all manner of innovative devices from half-track lorries for the War Office to six-wheeled buses for city corporations.

The car and commercial manufacturer Star was bought in 1928 and at about the same time, to signify the company's success, the Red Indian chief's head mascot 'Feathers in our cap' became Guy's talisman.

Buses and trolleybuses were taking an increasing share of the factory's output and it was firstly into these that Gardner diesel engines were fitted in the latter part of the decade, before they also found a place in the firm's lorries. With England emerging from recession in the early years of the 1930s the company announced various new lorries bearing names that would endure for 20 or more years: Wolf, Vixen, Warrior, Goliath and Otter. Before long, however, with some of Europe's

economies forging ahead, it became obvious that Germany was once again contemplating flexing its rejuvenated muscles.

From 1936 Guy worked on the development of various military vehicles such as the Ant and Lizard; a four wheel drive version of the Ant, the Quad-Ant, was subsequently produced in large numbers by Humber in Coventry. When war finally started, production was once again taken up by ministry contracts although a number of civilian versions of the Ant were made for bona fide trades.

Within a year of the war's end both bus and lorry production resumed, with improved versions of the pre-war range, and in 1948 Guy took over the Sunbeam Trolleybus Company, appropriately an offshoot of its founder's old firm, which had been started in 1929.

Traditionally, commercial vehicle cabs had been coachbuilt, with aluminium panels over a wood frame, but to ease production pressed steel was phased in around 1952, and in 1954 a new range of heavy lorries was introduced utilising AEC rolling chassis. These were initially named Goliath but a German firm of the same name, maker of some fairly ludicrous small-capacity cars and commercials since the 1930s, managed to make enough fuss to persuade a change of name to Invincible.

There was also a forward-control version of the Wolf, which would have resulted in a somewhat more cramped cockpit.

A completely new look, complete with fibreglass cabs, came in 1958, but this proved to be one feather too many and the ensuing downturn of the company's finances saw it being bought out by the somewhat unlikely Jaguar Cars in 1961.

Jaguar itself was destined to become part of the disastrous BMH empire three years later, but before this happened it oversaw the Big J heavy range, which reverted to steel cabs. When BMH was absorbed into British Leyland during 1968 the name Guy was kept

I am not entirely sure that the manufacturers were not a little naughty and slipped a pre-war Wolf truck into this brochure; be that as it may, the look was the same.

What an antediluvian looking cab, but look at the accessibility to the fuse box.

In those days Harrods was still posh.

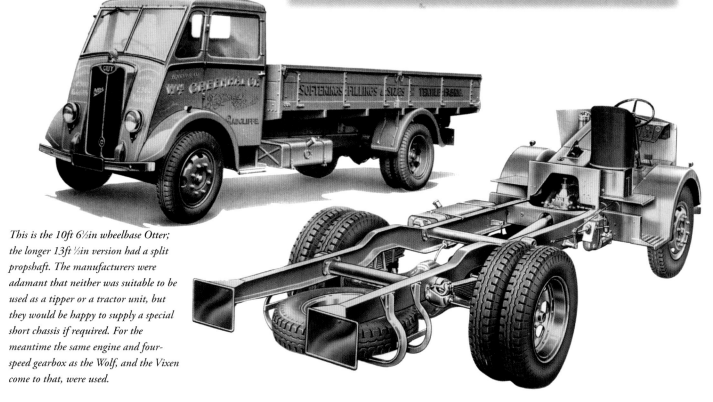

This is the 10ft 6½in wheelbase Otter; the longer 13ft ½in version had a split propshaft. The manufacturers were adamant that neither was suitable to be used as a tipper or a tractor unit, but they would be happy to supply a special short chassis if required. For the meantime the same engine and four-speed gearbox as the Wolf, and the Vixen come to that, were used.

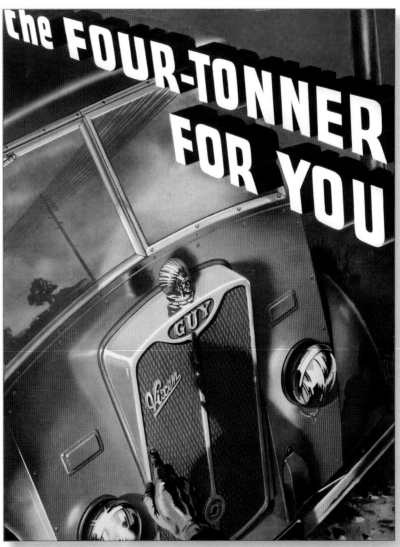

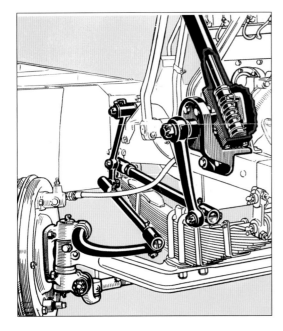

As on the Otter, this novel twin drag link steering was used.
It was claimed to give exceptionally light and steady control.

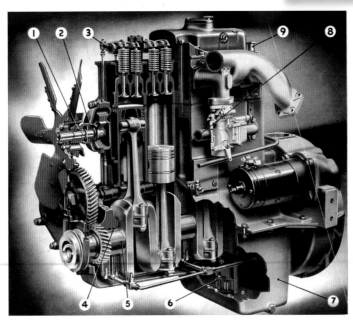

SPECIAL ENGINE FEATURES

1. Composite bearing and fan/pump spindle. Bearing is of generous dimensions and requires no attention during service.

2. Spring-loaded, rubber bonded carbon water pump seal.

3. Hollow rocker-shaft pressure lubricated from main oiling system.

4. Main bearing journals of 2⅛" diameter.

5. Dynamically balanced crankshaft machined from a heat-treated high tensile steel stamping.

6. Submerged gear type oil pump with safety valve to protect driving gear on camshaft from overload during low temperatures. Pump shrouded in gauze primary filter.

7. 12 pint capacity oil sump.

8. Water space.

9. External relief valve to reduce oil pressure and by-pass oil to the overhead valve mechanism.

The Vixen, contrary to the animal world, was larger than the Wolf and had a wheelbase of 13ft. The handsome radiator, as on other models, was of cast and polished aluminium.

Guy's all-purpose 3686cc engine.

Vehicles of this type were a familiar sight in large towns and cities before other methods were evolved to enable workmen to perform overhead construction and maintenance. This Vixen-based vehicle was built on a 10ft 6in wheelbase.

Height 19' 0"

The diesel Otter was announced towards the end of 1950. By now a tractor with 9ft 9in wheelbase was catalogued alongside with two longer chassis of 13ft and 14ft 9in. The gearbox was still a four-speed but a two-speed axle was offered. The slightly modernised cab was now quickly removable and was mounted on rubber silentblocs.

A new conception of economical Load-carrying ...

GUY DIESEL OTTER

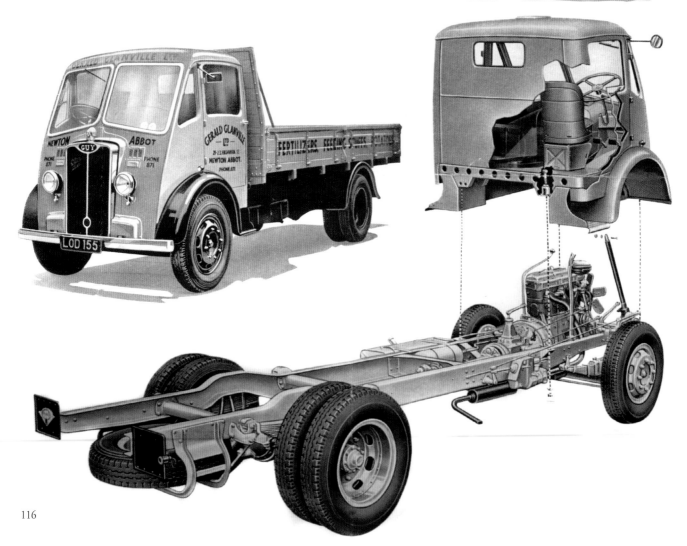

5.1 LITRE ENGINE

Bore 3.74" (95 mm.)	.	Stroke 4,725 (120 mm.)
Capacity . .	.	311.4 cu. ins. (5,103 c.c.)
R.A.C. rating .	. . . . .	33.5 h.p.
Maximum output	.	105 b.h.p. at 2,600 r.p.m.
Maximum torque	.	232 lb. ft. at 1,700 r.p.m.

GARDNER
4LK ENGINE

SPECIAL FEATURES OF THE ENGINE

1 **THERMOSTAT CONTROL.**—Returns water into suction side of pump until proper working temperature is attained. When temperature rises sufficiently the valve closes the by-pass and so forces all the water through the radiator.

2 **CYLINDER BLOCK.**—Cast in special ductile high-tensile cast-iron and fitted with dry type liners. Bolted to crank-case by large high tensile through bolts which also carry the main bearing caps.

3 **EXHAUSTER.**—Reciprocating piston type driven from crank fitted to valve camshaft.

4 **LUBRICATING OIL PUMP.**—Driven from camshaft by helical gears and vertical shaft. Internal gears of generous proportions to ensure satisfactory working and long life.

5 **VALVE CAMSHAFT.**—Chain-driven from crankshaft and carried by white metal bearings in crankcase. The composite construction allows removal of the cams for profile grinding.

6 **CONNECTING RODS.**—"H" section die-stampings in high tensile alloy steel and machined all over before being subjected to a 100% flaw detection inspection. Rifle drilled up to small end for pressure lubrication of gudgeon pin bush. Steel backed white metal big-end bearings.

7 **CRANKSHAFT.**—Accurately machined high tensile steel die stamping with large diameter hollow main and crank-pin journals joined by immensely stiff webs. Oil sealing screw threads cut in both ends of shaft.

8 **SUMP.**—Light, non-porous magnesium alloy casting fitted with primary oil filter and designed to prevent any sediment from reaching the oil pressure system.

9 **CRANKCASE.**—Cast in magnesium alloy, generously ribbed inside and outside and of exceptionally deep vertical section. The rigidity obviates concentrated loading and undue crankshaft deflection.

10 **GOVERNOR.**—Spring-loaded twin flyweight type. Load controlled by accelerator to vary engine speed and/or torque through linkage connecting governor to fuel pump. Ensures steady idling and maximum speeds and controls all intermediate speeds dependent upon position of accelerator.

11 **PISTONS.**—Cast in medium silicon aluminium alloy specially heat-treated to ensure consistent performance and of generous length to provide large bearing area which ensures minimum wear and oil consumption.

12 **FUEL INJECTION PUMP.**—C.A.V. Gardner-type with spring-loaded rams and tappets and individual priming levers. Fuel camshaft supported on large diameter ball-bearings, and driven by helical gears from valve camshaft. Driven gear on fuel camshaft free to slide on helical spline, providing automatic variation of injection timing. Automatic variation of timing with engine speed by means of yoke coupling the gear to the accelerator lever.

13 **CYLINDER HEADS.**—High tensile cast-iron with renewable hardened alloy iron valve seatings. Overhead valve mechanism pressure lubricated through hollow rocker shaft. Decompression mechanism provided to facilitate hand-starting and servicing adjustments.

14 **FUEL FILTER.**—Contains two gauze elements and incorporates a "leak-off" hole which permits escape of any air in pipe line on suction side and allows excess fuel to escape back to tank.

15 **AIR FILTER.**—Oil-bath type mounted in direct line with twin air streams from gauze protected ducts in front dash.

The Otter Mk III came with a wheelbase of 9ft 9in for tipper or tractor use and 13ft or 14ft 9in for haulage use. There was a choice of Gardner 4LK, Perkins P6 or 5.1-litre diesel engines; the former two were used in conjunction with a five-speed gearbox whilst the latter had a four-speed.

Almost straight out of the pages of the Eagle comic, the futuristically styled Invincible was visually light years away from Guy's products of less than 10 years previously. Four-wheelers came as a tipper with 8ft 9in wheelbase, tractor with 11ft 6in or truck with 15ft 6in or 17ft 9in. Six-wheelers came as a tractor or tipper with 11ft wheelbase, tipper or truck of 13ft 9in, and truck of 17ft 9in. The six-wheel twin-steer was available as trucks of 17ft 9in or 20ft, while the eight-wheeler was offered as a tipper with 13ft 9in wheelbase or a truck of 17ft 9in air brakes were standard.

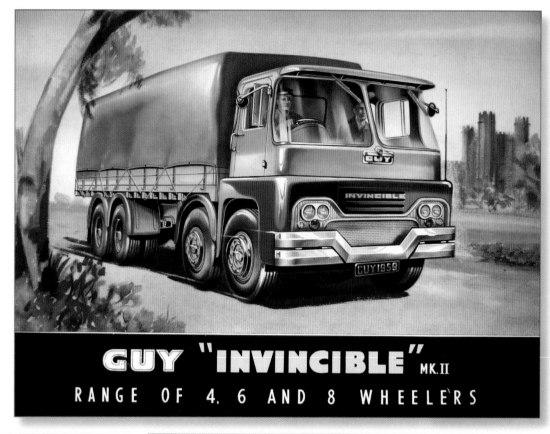

GUY "INVINCIBLE" MK.II
RANGE OF 4, 6 AND 8 WHEELERS

The extraordinary normal-control was only offered on four- or six-wheelers.

Power units were Gardner 6LW or 6LX, with the option of either 9.8-litre or 11.1-litre Leyland diesels. Five-speed gearboxes and Bendix-Westinghouse air brakes were standard.

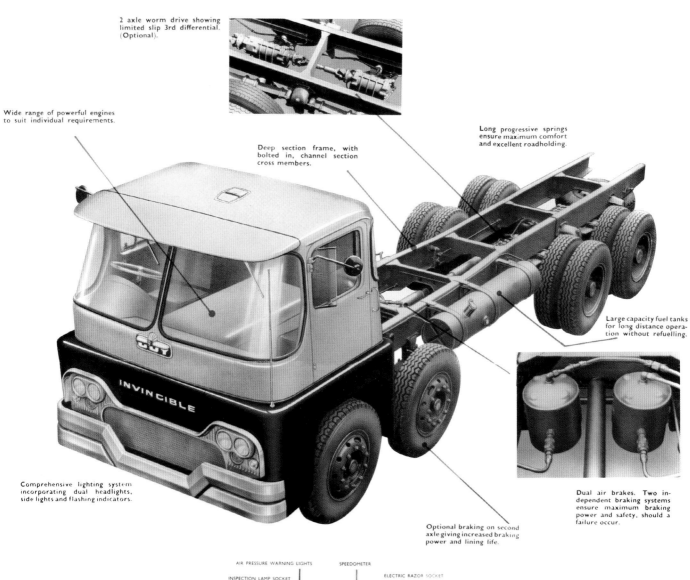

2 axle worm drive showing limited slip 3rd differential. (Optional).

Wide range of powerful engines to suit individual requirements.

Deep section frame, with bolted in, channel section cross members.

Long progressive springs ensure maximum comfort and excellent roadholding.

Large capacity fuel tanks for long distance operation without refuelling.

Comprehensive lighting system incorporating dual headlights, side lights and flashing indicators.

Dual air brakes. Two independent braking systems ensure maximum braking power and safety, should a failure occur.

Optional braking on second axle giving increased braking power and lining life.

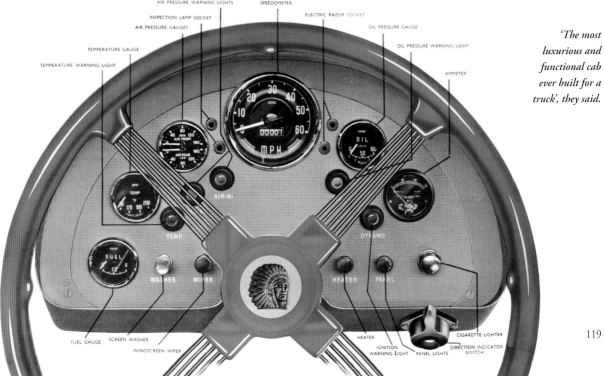

'The most luxurious and functional cab ever built for a truck', they said.

AIR PRESSURE WARNING LIGHTS
SPEEDOMETER
INSPECTION LAMP SOCKET
ELECTRIC RAZOR SOCKET
AIR PRESSURE GAUGES
OIL PRESSURE GAUGE
TEMPERATURE GAUGE
OIL PRESSURE WARNING LIGHT
TEMPERATURE WARNING LIGHT
AMMETER
FUEL GAUGE
SCREEN WASHER
WASHER
WIPER
HEATER
PANEL
DYNAMO
WINDSCREEN WIPER
HEATER
IGNITION WARNING LIGHT
PANEL LIGHTS
CIGARETTE LIGHTER
DIRECTION INDICATOR SWITCH

JENSEN

During the war years Jensen Motors, aside from their ministry contracts, busied itself with the development of a lightweight commercial vehicle. This was carried out with the assistance of the Reynolds Tube Company, and various prototypes were completed using aluminium for the main structure.

As soon as the war was over the firm went into production with two aluminium-framed models, a pantechnicon and an open truck, both powered by the ubiquitous Perkins P6 diesel engine. A few coaches were also built using the same basic structure but, in spite of the Jensen's futuristic attributes, it did not fit in with the way that commercial vehicles were perceived, and in 1956 it was quietly dropped.

Alongside its white elephant Jensen also produced a diminutive articulated lorry, the Jen-Tug, which was powered by Ford's 1172cc sidevalve petrol engine and weighed in at 30cwt unladen. A few of these were made around 1950 which relied on battery/electric power, but the problems associated with that mode of propulsion led the firm up another blind alley. It then concentrated on the petrol version, which was later fitted with a BMC petrol engine, or the same firm's 2.2-litre diesel, so that it could cope with a greater payload.

The Jen-Tug remained in production until 1959 and thereafter, until 1962, the firm built the German Tempo under licence. This was a small commercial with a possible payload of just over 1-ton which featured an Austin engine and front-wheel drive.

"JNSN" LIGHTWEIGHT DIESEL COMMERCIAL VEHICLE
SPECIFICATION

ENGINE
Type : Perkins Diesel P.6, six cylinders.
Bore : $3\frac{1}{2}$ in.
Stroke : 5 in.
B.H.P. : 70 at 2,200 r.p.m.
Max. Torque : 184 lbs. ft. at 1,000 r.p.m.
Electric pre-heater and Kigass injector for easy starting from cold.

CLUTCH
Borg & Beck dry single plate, 12 in. diameter.

GEARBOX
Five speeds forward and reverse. Provision for power take-off.

Ratios :			
1st	...	...	6.55—1
2nd	...	...	3.60—1
3rd	...	...	1.81—1
4th (normal top)			1.00—1
5th (overdrive)			.81—1
Reverse	...		5.00—1

TRANSMISSION
Open propeller shaft with two intermediate bearings.

SPRINGS
Semi-elliptic, rubber insulated. Front, 43 in. centres ; rear, 62 in. centres.

FRONT AXLE
Drop forged, one section beam.

REAR AXLE
Spiral bevel, fully floating. Ratio : 7 to 1.

LUBRICATION
Tecalemit, pressure controlled to each individual point, actuated by clutch pedal.

STANDARD SUPERSTRUCTURE
Corrugated alloy loading platform with timber inserts, detachable drop sides and tail.

BRAKES
Two leading shoe (Girling), 16 in. diameter, hydraulic application.

STEERING
Cam gears, fore and aft drag link.

WHEELS AND TYRES
34 in. by 7 in. R.H.S. Dunlop. Single front, twin rear.

FUEL TANK
Twenty gallons capacity. Snap-on filler cap. Visual gauge calibrated in gallons

LIGHTING
C.A.V. "De Luxe." Two headlamps, two side lamps, two rear lamps. Roof light in cab. "Stop" lamp and "Pass" light. Dipping : Split reflector.

STARTER
C.A.V. 12 volt axial type.

BATTERY
12 volt, 120 amp. hours.

DYNAMO
Lucas 12 volt, 140 watt.

EQUIPMENT
Electric windscreen wiper.
Full kit of tools.
Front number plate.
Special recess for rear number plate.
Spare wheel and tyre.
Hydraulic jack.
Two driving mirrors
Trafficators.
Driver's seat adjustable vertically and horizontally.

DIMENSIONS AND WEIGHTS

	Standard	Short Wheel Base
Wheel base ...	16 ft. 2 in.	12 ft. $8\frac{1}{2}$ in.
Track	6 ft. 1 in.	6 ft. 1 in.
Overall length ...	27 ft. 6 in.	22 ft. $6\frac{1}{2}$ in.
Overall width ...	7 ft. 6 in.	7 ft. 6 in.
Loading platform	23 ft. × 7 ft.	18 ft. × 7 ft.
Unladen weight ...	58 cwts.	56 cwts.
Pay load	Up to 6 tons	Up to 6 tons
Tyre rating (gross)	8 tons 5 cwts.	8 tons 5 cwts.

There has never been a lorry, before or since, with such clean lines in profile.

An all-alloy pantechnicon with a capacity of 1632 cubic feet was also available on the same chassis. One was languishing in a field not five miles from the publishers of this book until the early 1970s.

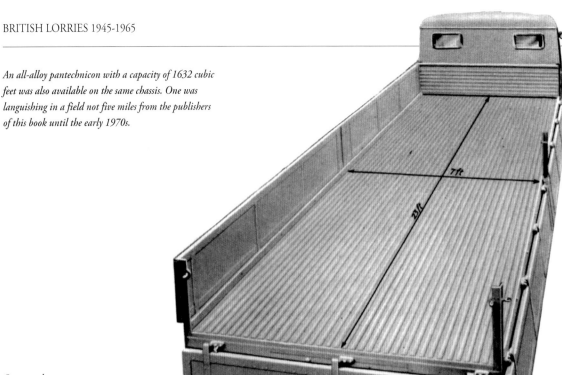

Some modern motor manufacturers should take a good look at these photographs from very nearly 60 years ago.

JNSN SPECIAL FEATURES

GENERAL

Permitted speed, 30 m.p.h.

Bulk capacity loads up to 6 tons.

Unladen weight of flat platform lorry, 56 cwts.

Area of loading platform, 23 ft. × 7 ft.

Main frame and superstructure (corresponding to the orthodox "Chassis and Body") constructed in one unit of specially selected high duty alloys throughout.

ECONOMY

Six-cylinder Diesel engine, combining high efficiency with low fuel consumption and long life. Electric pre-heater and Kigass injector provide easy starting in the coldest weather.

Special engine mounting allows engine to be withdrawn from front of vehicle as a complete unit, with water and exhaust systems, filters, etc., intact (Patent Nos. 588948, 600755). See illustrations on this page.

Heavy duty 5-speed gear box, incorporating overdrive top gear and provision for power take-off.

Automatic chassis lubrication by Tecalemit system of multiple pumps actuated by clutch pedal, providing an individual feed to each point.

Rubber insulated spring mountings.

Can be used with impunity on rough and uneven ground.

Basic properties of the alloys and the method of construction provide for torsional flexibility far exceeding that possessed by the conventional load carrier.

Complete immunity from rust and corrosion.

COMFORT AND SAFETY

Visibility from driver's seat exceptionally good in all directions.

Comfortable seat for the driver, adjustable horizontally and vertically.

Easy steering and good lock provide excellent manœuvrability.

Position of pedals and controls ensures maximum comfort and freedom from fatigue.

Ventilation of cab adjustable for cold or warm air.

Top half of driver's windscreen can be fully opened.

Unrestricted entrance to cab with a " Grab Rail " on either side.

C.A.V. " De Luxe " electrical equipment.

KARRIER

The Yorkshire firm of Clayton, using the name Karrier from the outset, commenced building commercial vehicles during 1907. Up to and including the First World War it produced, apart from a light truck, two models, the A and B types, both of which could be adapted for passenger use or variously carry goods weighing up to 5 tons.

In 1920 the firm became known simply as Karrier Motors Ltd and a development of its wartime light truck, given increased capacity, was introduced, with forward-control variants following rapidly.

The following years saw further diversification when the firm added trolleybuses to its range during 1928. From an outsider's viewpoint the Depression was being successfully weathered and, in addition to larger lorries of up to 12-ton capacity and further passenger vehicles, Karrier came up with a novel three-wheeled mechanical horse with quickly detachable trailer, pre-dating the better-known Scammell version. This had been developed at the instigation of the London, Midland & Scottish Railway, who were keen to find an easily manoeuvrable and commodious vehicle for urban parcels delivery to replace their largely horsedrawn fleet.

Things were not as rosy as they seemed, however, and in 1934, following the calling in of the receivers, Karrier became the property of the Rootes empire. The next year a move was made to Commer's Luton factory, where Karrier produced the smaller commercials for general and municipal use as well as its own little tractor units such as the three-wheeled Colt, shortly joined by a four-wheeler named the Bantam.

War work included four wheel drive gun tractors and medium trucks as well as Bantams for use within

The "BANTAM" TRACTOR

WITH AUTOMATIC COUPLING GEAR
HAULS A FIVE-TON PAY LOAD
ON TRAILERS OF THE QUICKLY-DETACHABLE TYPE

EQUIPPED WITH 'BK' TYPE COUPLING GEAR

Makes short work of the short haul!
THE "BANTAM" TRACTOR

"BANTAM" TRACTOR
EQUIPPED WITH 'J' TYPE COUPLING GEAR

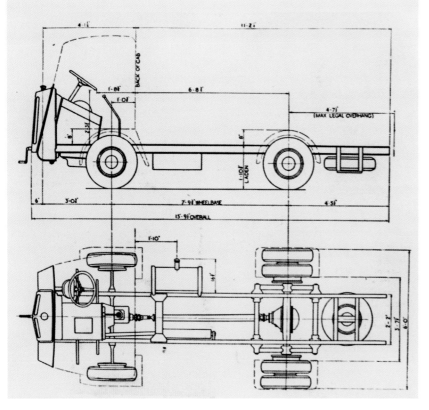

the services. With the cessation of hostilities Bantams for commercial use were put back into full production in company with the pre-war 3- to 4-tonner. The latter was renamed the Gamecock for 1950, and when Commer began to use the TS two-stroke diesel it became available as an optional power plant. Little further in the way of visual modernisation took place until the late 1950s, when divided windscreens gave way to single-pane versions. Around the same time the firm made a number of battery electric Bantams, named the Electric Karrier, in conjunction with Smiths Delivery Vehicles Ltd. These were used for refuse collection in towns and cities in a bid to cut noise and pollution but sadly, despite much talk, little further constructive has been done along the same lines since.

In 1961 Commer came up with their Walk-Thru delivery vehicle, which was also sold as a Karrier, and a year or so later the Bantam underwent a degree of modernisation in order to keep it current. Some of the heavier Commers were by now available as Karriers due to the demand for larger municipal vehicles, a role for which Karrier was well known. This continued once the two firms had come under Chrysler ownership: the name of Karrier was to continue whilst Commer was eventually done away with.

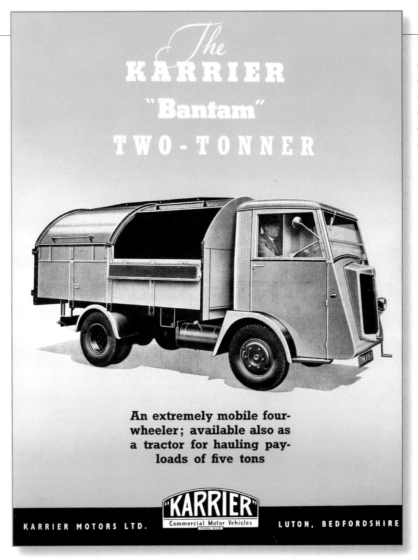

Municipal vehicles were considered an important part of the Karrier's output, as evidenced by a dustcart appearing on the cover of their May 1946 brochure.

With a turning circle of under 30ft for normal models and under 25ft for the tractor the Bantams were certainly manoeuvrable. Both had a 2-litre petrol engine and four-wheel hydraulic brakes.

125

A maid of all work for the well-equipped local authority including three varieties of the all important dustcart from 7 to 12 cubic yards, the largest being of the moving floor variety. Supplied in primer as standard, they could be painted and signwritten if required. Engine size was up to 2266cc with the new model Bantam.

DRIVER'S CAB. With a distinguished modern appearance the full forward cab of all steel construction, has an effective interior width of 61 ins. The seats are well upholstered and embody sponge rubber cushions, the driver's seat being of the bucket type whilst that for the passenger is so designed as to accommodate two if required. Easy entry is afforded through 35 ins. front-hinged doors, set well forward and provided with convenient steps. Doors have fixed quarter lights with quick lift lever-controlled full opening drop windows in toughened safety glass, and both can be locked. All controls are carefully positioned to ensure maximum driving comfort with minimum fatigue. Ideal driving conditions are further assisted by easily visible instruments, wide vision two-piece screen of toughened glass with dual electric screen wipers, fully insulated cab roof and effective sealing against draughts. One large pocket is built into the fascia, and a 6 watt roof light gives adequate illumination. Engine servicing is facilitated by the provision of quick release traps in engine cover, giving access to all important maintenance points. This cover, when required, can be easily removed, being held in position by quick release catches. Driving mirror and licence holder are supplied with cab, which is supported on the frame by four large rubber mountings.

The perfect shop on wheels!

HOME SERVICE

HYGIENIC MOBILE SHOP

KARRIER 'BANTAM' WITH DIESEL OR CHROME BORE PETROL ENGINE

A ROOTES PRODUCT

The mobile shop was very much something of the times. They were often seen around the large postwar housing estates which were springing up and which usually had inadequate shopping facilities.

Better than another branch !

Reduces labour cost in relation to turnover.
Earns the loyalty and goodwill of the housewife.
Attractive displays encourage 'impulse' buying'.
Trade-right, coachbuilt bodies with lasting, hygienic,
easy to clean finish and fittings.

Save as you serve

Karrier offered a very comprehensive package which, in addition to custom fitted interiors, ranged from the provision of Smith's Insulated Cold Storage cabinets to an SWF Musical Horn: 'A pleasant and distinctive warning signal to advise the presence of the vehicle – "Take it from Here", "Come to the Cookhouse Door", and other attractive tunes to customers requirements'.

The Gamecock was Karrier's answer for users who wanted a larger-capacity vehicle than the Bantam but one which retained all its features such as low loading height and manoeuvrability.

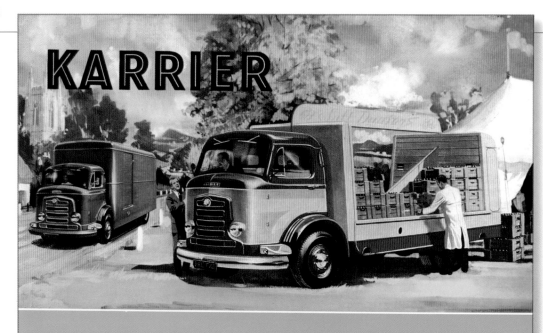

KARRIER

"GAMECOCK" 3-4 TON MODELS

PETROL OR DIESEL

ROOTES PRODUCTS

You could take your choice of their own seven main bearing, six-cylinder petrol engine which they were proud to advertise as having 'porous chrome bores' which would 'guarantee phenomenal life' or, if your preference was for a diesel, a Perkins Six-354.

Leading dimensions

	PETROL	DIESEL
Engine	6 cyl. 'underfloor' o.h.v.	6 cyl. horizontal 'Six-354'
Displacement	4750 c.c.	5800 c.c.
Maximum power (gross)	91 b.h.p. @ 2600 r.p.m.	97 b.h.p. @ 2600 r.p.m.
Torque	216 lb. ft. @ 1200 r.p.m.	225 lb. ft. @ 1350 r.p.m.

Gearbox ratios:		
Top	direct	
3rd	1·838 : 1	
2nd	3·478 : 1	
1st	7·227 : 1	
Reverse	8·431 : 1	

	PETROL	DIESEL
Rear axle ratio:	5·43 : 1	4·88 : 1
Theoretical maximum road speed with standard tyres (27 × 6) and axle ratio:	40·7 m.p.h.	45·4 m.p.h.
Theoretical gradient climbable, laden, based on a rolling resistance of 30 lb. per ton, with 27 × 6 tyres and standard rear axle ratio:	1 in 2½	1 in 2½

	SHORT WHEELBASE	LONG WHEELBASE
Wheelbase	115 in.	141 in.
Wheeltrack:		
Front (at the ground)	74¼ in.	74¼ in.
Rear	64 in.	64 in.
Overall height of cab (laden) 27 × 6 tyres	87 $\frac{7}{16}$ in.	87 $\frac{7}{16}$ in.
Turning circle (approx.)	44 ft. 0 in.	51 ft. 0 in.
Fuel tank capacity	16 gallons	16 gallons

	PETROL cwt.	DIESEL cwt.	PETROL cwt.	DIESEL cwt.
Approx. chassis weight (less fuel, water and spare wheel)	40½	42¾	41	43½
Approx. chassis/cab weight (less fuel, water and spare wheel)	43¾	46¼	44½	47
Allowance for fuel, water and spare wheel	2¾	3	2¾	3

KARRIER

'BANTAM' 4-5 TON TRACTOR

PETROL OR DIESEL   *A ROOTES PRODUCT*

That the original Bantam concept had been right is evidenced by the 1959 versions, but by this time the turning circle had gone down to 28ft.

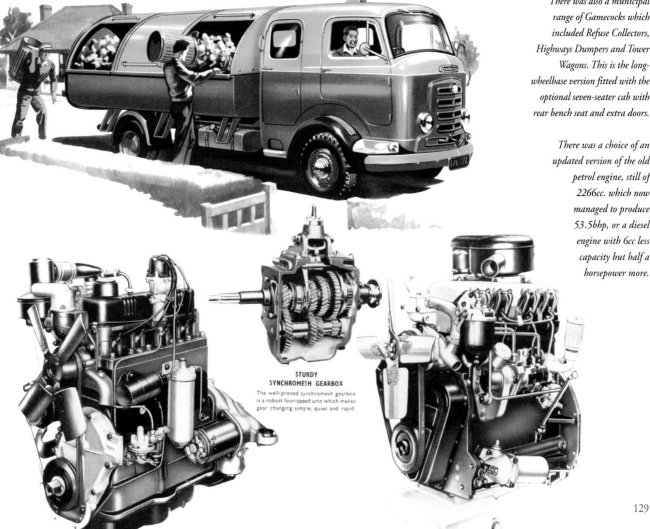

STURDY SYNCHROMESH GEARBOX

The well-proved synchromesh gearbox is a robust four-speed unit which makes gear changing simple, quiet and rapid.

There was also a municipal range of Gamecocks which included Refuse Collectors, Highways Dumpers and Tower Wagons. This is the long-wheelbase version fitted with the optional seven-seater cab with rear bench seat and extra doors.

There was a choice of an updated version of the old petrol engine, still of 2266cc. which now managed to produce 53.5bhp, or a diesel engine with 6cc less capacity but half a horsepower more.

'This form of vehicle enables the motive unit to be continuously employed with one or more of its attendant semi-trailers whilst the remainder are being loaded or unloaded; a system of shuttle transport with an endless variety of applications. Incidentally, no extra road tax has to be paid for the extra semi-trailers used', read the brochure. Sounds like sense to me, and after all the Bantam was only ever intended to operate over short to medium distances.

To the modern driver the glowing terms used to describe the manner in which his predecessors were catered for might appear fanciful, but the Karrier range would have been quite pleasant, if sluggish, to drive compared with some commercials at the time. It does not mention here, however, that the cab was supported on the chassis by four large rubber mountings. The manufacturers were also quite generous in that they threw in a pair of driving mirrors, rubber floor mat with felt underlay and a licence holder.

DRIVER COMFORT MEANS SAFETY AND EFFICIENCY

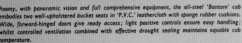

Roomy, with panoramic vision and full comprehensive equipment, the all-steel 'Bantam' cab embodies two well-upholstered bucket seats in 'P.V.C.' leathercloth with sponge rubber cushions. Wide, forward-hinged doors give ready access; light positive controls ensure easy handling; whilst controlled ventilation combined with effective draught sealing maintains equable cab temperature.

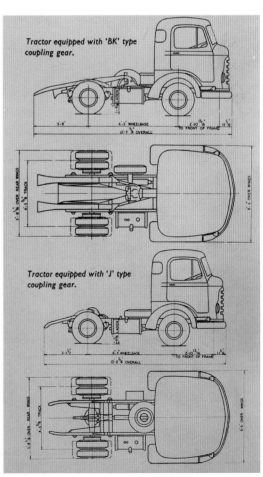

Tractor equipped with 'BK' type coupling gear.

Tractor equipped with 'J' type coupling gear.

LEYLAND

EL COMET DE
Leyland

UN VEHICULO PARA
SERVICIOS PESADOS
DISEÑADO Y FABRICADO PARA LOS
MERCADOS DEL MUNDO POR
Leyland Motors
-Ltd-
LOS FABRICANTES VANGUARDISTAS
DE VEHICULOS EN LA GRAN BRETAÑA

Para Transportes Económicos

Export was all-important in the immediate postwar years: here is the brochure that prospective customers for the Comet range of trucks, tippers and tractors would have been given by the Buenos Aires Leyland Agent in 1949.

Taking its name from the town where it was situated the firm of Leyland, formed in 1908, was an amalgam of two firms, Lancashire Steam Motors and Leyland-Crossley. Until 1909 its steam lorries were chain driven, but at that point a shaft-drive chassis was introduced which was suitable for either steam or petrol engines. In 1912 a three-ton lorry was submitted for trials by the War Office and, after completing these successfully, was certificated for the subsidy scheme that the government was running in the years immediately leading up to the First World War.

A good many manufacturers took advantage of this government incentive to build vehicles suitable for use by the armed forces, and were rewarded with a set amount of money per unit

Leyland produced a large number of these 3-tonners during the war. They became known as the RAF type as the majority of them were used in that branch of the services. After the war, with a glut of ex-ministry vehicles adversely affecting sales of new vehicles, Leyland bought back a large number of 3-tonners to recondition and sell so that they could at least profit from this section of the market.

Steam lorry production had been halted during the war but was recommenced in 1920 as an alternative to the range of petrol-driven trucks and passenger vehicles, ranging from 30cwt to 6 tons, that were now leaving the factory.

The introduction of what proved to be an extremely successful range of passenger chassis including the Lion and Lioness during 1925 led to the cessation, one year later, of steam lorry production, the surplus from that side of the business being sold off to Atkinson, just up the road at Preston. The new range marked the beginning of the firm's predilection for felines and, contrastingly, herbivores as suitable names for their products; over the next 40 or so years Leyland was to

This is the 75bhp six-cylinder 5-litre diesel engine with a seven main bearing crankshaft. Leyland made much of the use of pre-finished cylinder liners, which allowed replacement by hand with the engine in situ. There was an optional 100bhp petrol version which was generally similar to the diesel apart from its ancillaries and the specifications of certain components. The gearbox had five speeds.

The semi-forward-control Comet came in three forms: the Haulage with 14ft 2 in wheelbase, the Tipper with 10ft 5in wheelbase and the Tractor with 9ft 2 in wheelbase. The electrical system was 24 volts on diesel models and the wiring was made up in separate, quickly detachable, harness assemblies.

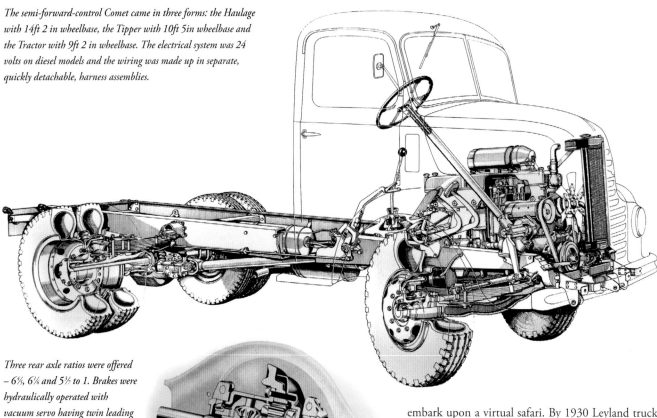

Three rear axle ratios were offered – 6⅗, 6⅕ and 5⅗ to 1. Brakes were hydraulically operated with vacuum servo having twin leading shoes and a lining area of 450sq in.

An alternative rear axle was available with two speeds selected by means of vacuum servo. The high ratio was obtained through a bevel and crown wheel and the low ratio through epicyclic gearing.

embark upon a virtual safari. By 1930 Leyland trucks, for example, ranged from 2½ to 12 tons and from Beaver to Hippo. This was also the year Leyland began to produce its first diesel engines.

The 1930s saw the expansion of the passenger vehicle side of the business but this did not stop Leyland from adding further trucks to the range, including the perversely but appropriately named eight-wheeler Octopus during 1934, the semi-forward-control Lynx and fire appliances.

With war on the horizon Leyland had developed specialised trucks under contract to the government, the Retriever 6x4 and a military version of the Lynx 6-tonner, so from September 1939 output of these was stepped up. The Retriever, in particular, was supplied in many guises, from mobile wireless or searchlight units to crane and bridging applications. The firm was also called upon to manufacture much other material, including tank engines, and to maintain a steady output of vehicles for civilian use, and from 1941 tank assembly began to take place within the factory. Towards the end of 1942 existing contracts were allowed to run out and the whole factory was turned over to the production of Centaur and Cromwell tanks as well as, from 1943, the design and eventual production of the Comet. From 1944 there was a partial resumption of truck production when the militarised Hippo Mk II began to be made.

The first new postwar truck to be announced was

the 5/7-ton Comet, in 1947, followed a year later by restyled versions of some of the old faithfuls such as the Beaver and Octopus.

Although Leyland was increasingly involved in the development and production of passenger vehicles, the company in no way neglected opportunities to expand in other directions. The Scottish commercial vehicle firm of Albion was bought in 1951 and then, four years later, Scammell was added to the portfolio. At first both these firms were left to carry on much as they had been, with their own persona, but by the end of the decade Albions were increasingly looking like Leylands under another name.

Another important acquisition, during 1961, was Standard-Triumph, which resulted in some of the Standard commercials henceforth being marketed under the Leyland badge.

The following year Leyland and AEC agreed to a merger, out of which was created the increasingly unwieldy Leyland Motor Corporation, but it was not until 1964 that any significant new models appeared, in the form of the Freightline series.

During the later part of the 1960s Leyland continued to take over various other manufacturers, including Rover in 1967. One year later the group took the step that was ultimately to prove its undoing when it merged with the British Motor Corporation to form the British Leyland Motor Corporation.

All manner of fresh passenger vehicles and commercials were brought into production the next few years

SENSITIVE CONTROLS

Adjustable pedals, balanced controls, and well-raked steering column ensure effortless control and comfort. The brake pedal is directly coupled to the air-pressure control-valve, giving sensitive operation of the powerful brakes.

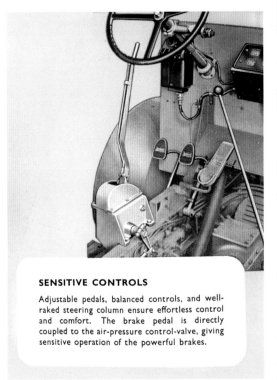

EASY BRAKE ADJUSTMENT

Mounted directly over the king pins, the front air pressure brake cylinders are fitted with easily-manipulated thumb screws which allow fine brake adjustment. The tension side of the road spring leaves is shot blasted to increase their resistance to fatigue and prolong their life under heavy service.

Strictly for export, the twin-axle Super Beaver was available as a Tractor with 11ft wheelbase, a Tipper with 12ft 6in wheelbase and Haulage with 16ft 9in wheelbase. The three-axle Super Hippo had a 14ft 6in wheelbase in Tractor form, 15ft 6in as a Tipper and 17ft 9in for Haulage. All were fitted with a six-cylinder diesel engine of 9.8 litres developing just over 125bhp and coupled to a five-speed gearbox. Certain Haulage models and all Tractors in the Super Hippo series were fitted with an auxiliary gearbox with step up or down ratio of 1.328 to 1.

Although Leyland was to buy Scammell during 1955 the two firms had been involved in joint ventures for some while, as is evidenced by this 1952 brochure. On to the trailer is being loaded one of Scammell's famous rocking-beam axle units, which they had developed during the 1920s.

Provides the perfect link-up

The Hippo (far right) of 1958 still had a steel cab with two-piece windscreen. By now an alternative diesel engine of 11.1 litres, producing 150bhp, was available.

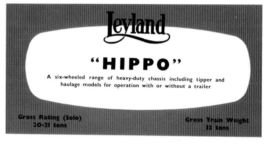

Standard Types of SCAMMELL Semi Trailers . . .

. . . available for Coupling to the LEYLAND Tractor

Leyland

"HIPPO"

A six-wheeled range of heavy-duty chassis including tipper and haulage models for operation with or without a trailer

Gross Rating (Solo) 20-21 tons

Gross Train Weight 32 tons

The two ramps which take the flanged wheels of the trailer part of the coupling gear are bolted to the special tractor frame.

The retractable undercarriage at the front end of the trailer permits instant coupling between tractor and trailer.

The standard rear bogie (far right) consisted of two driven axles with overhead worm drives which were linked together by a short universal-jointed propeller shaft, but home market models could be supplied with a bogie comprising one undriven axle for solo work only.

Double-driven rear axle

SIMPLE ENGINE REMOVAL
All-round access to Power Unit

Leyland COMET
(12 TON RANGE)

with the modern all steel 'Vista-Vue' cab

and extra powerful brakes for safety at speed

LUXURY CAB WITH CAR COMFORT

The modern Leyland "Vista-Vue" cab offers driving comfort far superior to that normally provided on commercial vehicles. Its double skin with glass-fibre insulation . . . Dunlopillo seats in hard-wearing attractive Vynide . . . all-round visibility with twin rainbow screen wipers . . . flexible spring loaded cab mountings . . . well-placed controls coupled with lightness of steering ; all contribute to banish tension by eliminating driving strain and effort. Extra long distances can be covered with ease in a "Vista-Vue" cab. Luxuries available for relaxed driving include a built-in radio, and a de-luxe heating and ventilating system incorporating a powerful de-mister for the wrap-round windscreen.

ALL-ROUND VISION

The "Vista-Vue" cab with wrap-round windscreen has a total glazing area of approximately 3,000 sq. in. (19,355 sq. cm.). This, together with swivelling quarter lights and full drop winding windows, supplemented by a central rear window with curved quarter lights on either side, ensure perfect all-round visibility.

but the whole sorry conglomerate began to fail owing to a combination of management ineptitude and resolute trade unions. In 1975 the government gave it a massive cash injection and took overall control.

Although other marques within the family died at this point, or within the next few years, Leyland lived on, producing trucks and passenger vehicles until 1986 when the truck side was sold to DAF. Two years later the bus business went to Volvo. Leyland trucks are made to this day but have been owned since 1998 by PACCAR.

The 1959 Comet range consisted of six models. Haulage versions had a choice of three wheelbase – 13ft 7in, 14ft 8in and 16ft 11in. The Tipper's wheelbase was 9ft 10in, the tractor's wheelbase was 8ft 1in and the Scammell Tractor's was 8ft. Although the gross laden weight was 12 tons the Tractor models used with semi-trailers were rated at 18 tons.
The standard engine fitted to the Comet was the Leyland 350 six-cylinder diesel, which developed 100bhp, but Tractors had the slightly larger-capacity Leyland 375 with an extra 10bhp. The manufacturers confidently predicted a mileage of 200,000 between overhauls.

By 1960 the Octopus was increasingly sophisticated and could even be ordered with two varieties of rear suspension (as could the Hippo): the traditional trunnion-mounted rigid bogie riding on semi-elliptic leaf springs combined with torque rods; or non-reactive bell crank lever suspension, also on semi elliptic springs, which was considered more suitable for the higher speeds possible on the improving trunk roads of the time. There was also a choice of 5-, 6- or even 7-speed gearboxes, the latter two by way of an overdrive sixth speed or an additional crawler gear. Haulage models came in two wheelbases: 14ft 9in or 17ft, Tippers being available only on the shorter one.

The new Leyland easy-access cab is available as an all-steel unit or with glass fibre reinforced panels.

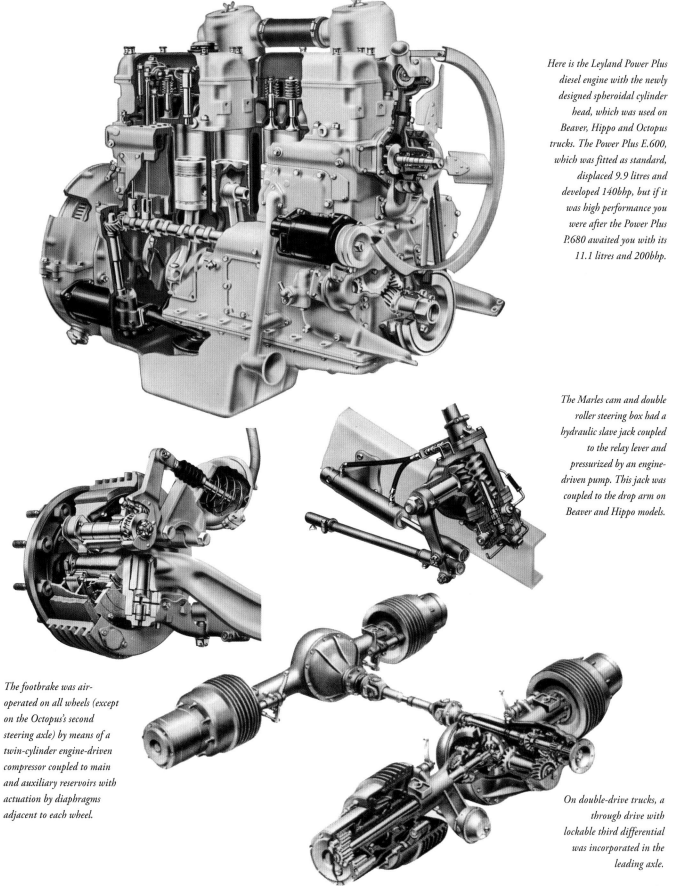

Here is the Leyland Power Plus diesel engine with the newly designed spheroidal cylinder head, which was used on Beaver, Hippo and Octopus trucks. The Power Plus E.600, which was fitted as standard, displaced 9.9 litres and developed 140bhp, but if it was high performance you were after the Power Plus P.680 awaited you with its 11.1 litres and 200bhp.

The Marles cam and double roller steering box had a hydraulic slave jack coupled to the relay lever and pressurized by an engine-driven pump. This jack was coupled to the drop arm on Beaver and Hippo models.

The footbrake was air-operated on all wheels (except on the Octopus's second steering axle) by means of a twin-cylinder engine-driven compressor coupled to main and auxiliary reservoirs with actuation by diaphragms adjacent to each wheel.

On double-drive trucks, a through drive with lockable third differential was incorporated in the leading axle.

The 1962 Comet had the Leyland 370 diesel engine of just over 6 litres and 110bhp. Haulage model came in three wheelbases: 13ft 7in, 14ft 8in and 16ft 11in. The Tipper had a wheelbase of 9ft 10in and the Tractor either 8ft or 8ft 1in.

The Super Comet for the same year had the Leyland 400 diesel engine of a little over 6½ litres, producing 125bhp. Both Comets had a five-speed gearbox. A sixth speed was available as an option, as was a two-speed rear axle.

1962 Hippo and Beaver trucks had the Leyland 600 motor as standard, with the 680 unit an option (standard on lhd chassis). The Hippo was 20 tons gross solo or 32 tons gross train weight. There were two haulage wheelbases of 14ft 9in and 17ft, a tipper of 12ft 6in and a dumper of 11ft.

The Beaver was rated at 14 tons gross in haulage form, with three wheelbase options - 13ft 6in, 15ft or 17ft 6in. Also offered were an 8ft wheelbase tractor and a tipper with 12ft wheelbase. In common with other Vista View cab models, a fibreglass cab was offered as an alternative with a weight saving of 1¾cwt.

MAUDSLAY

When the Maudslay Motor Company was set up in 1901 the family had already amassed around 100 years of experience in the field of engineering. The founder's grandfather, Henry Maudslay was working at Woolwich Arsenal when, in the same year as Nelson fought the battle of Trafalgar, he invented the micrometer, going on to produce something that was arguably far more important.

Until that time it had not been possible to produce screw threads with much degree of accuracy, and the attendant lack of interchangability and the laborious process of matching made assembly and disassembly an irksome task. Henry Maudslay's invention and development of an accurate screw-cutting lathe was to put an end to all that. It was no coincidence that the Whitworth thread was so called: Whitworth had been one of Maud-

An atmospheric piece of artwork of a Maudslay Mogul at work.

slay's apprentices and went on to continue the work that his master had begun on thread standardisation.

Even after Maudslay's death in 1831 the firm he had founded was synonymous with some of the great names and projects in the heady days of the industrial revolution. Maudslay engines went into Brunel's ship *Great Western* and into what was most probably the world's first motor-powered commercial road vehicle, Charles Dance's steam carriage of the 1830s.

A downturn in the marine engine business at the end of the 19th century led to a change of direction by Henry's grandson W H Maudslay and to a move from London to Coventry, where Maudslay joined dozens of firms involved in the motor manufacturing business in the first years of the 20th century. A year or two later W H's son Reginald was instrumental in setting up the

Standard Motor Company, which was to last in various guises right through to the sad demise of the British motor industry in the last quarter of the 20th century.

Primarily Maudslay set out to build private cars, fitted with overhead camshaft engines of their own manufacture, but within a year or two they were marketing a derivative of these chassis as a commercial.

CAB. Full forward control, ample screen area and narrow pillars plus a well arranged driving position permit safe and easy handling.

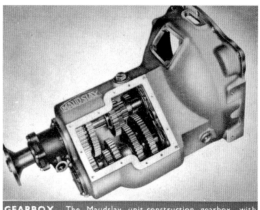

GEARBOX. The Maudslay unit-construction gearbox, with five forward speeds, allows fullest advantage to be taken of engine power under all operating conditions.

The Mogul Tipper was available with either side or rear tipping. Wheelbase was 10ft 9½in.

ENGINE. The A.E.C., 7·7 litre, six cylindered compression ignition engine, developing 98 h.p., provides ample power for all operating conditions.

FRONT AXLE. Forged from the finest grade steel the "H" section front axle is specially designed to resist front wheel braking stresses. Brake adjustment is unaffected by steering movement.

Although their early attempts met with an occasional bulk order, and even a design award or two, production was spasmodic, with the firm concentrating on the private car side. Things changed somewhat with the introduction of two fresh models in 1912, a 30cwt and 3-tonner, which arrived at just the right time for the firm to take advantage of government contracts for commercials to be supplied during the war. Such was the demand for the 3-tonner that it even ended up being additionally produced by Rover to ensure adequate supplies.

The postwar decade saw heavier commercials emanating from the factory, the largest, a 10-ton six-wheeler, taking to the roads in the less than happy year of 1929. The firm had ceased the manufacture of private cars many years before, and so it was down to commercials and passenger vehicles to see it through the difficult years of the early 1930s. Maudslay nearly went

down during 1935, but by 1939 it had been refinanced and had brought fresh products to the market place with wheel options ranging from from four to eight and lovely names such as Mogul, Maharajah and Mikado.

World War II saw production of the Mogul maintained for civilian users and an armed forces version of the same named the Militant.

Gilbert and Sullivan must have been considered old hat postwar as the Mikado became known as the Meritor and an Indian lady was introduced into the range, the Maharanee, as well as a six-wheeled twin-steering vehicle named the Mustang.

The company's long heritage did not stop it being engulfed by AEC during 1948, and although at first most current models continued in production, within three years the manufacture of pure Maudslays was to cease, Although it was possible to buy a Maudslay in 1960, they were little more than rebadged AECs.

The AEC 9.6-litre diesel engine developed 125bhp at 1,800rpm and had a one-piece cylinder block fitted with dry liners, the design incorporated a pair of cylinder heads, each covering three cylinders. In common with various other diesel-engined commercials the dynamo and starter were 24-volt but headlamps and other ancillaries were 12-volt.

Rear axles were overhead worm drive. On the Meritor the dual drive axles were interconnected by a short, universally-jointed shaft with a third differential built into the first axle. The semi-elliptic springs were interconnected by freely swinging balance beams.

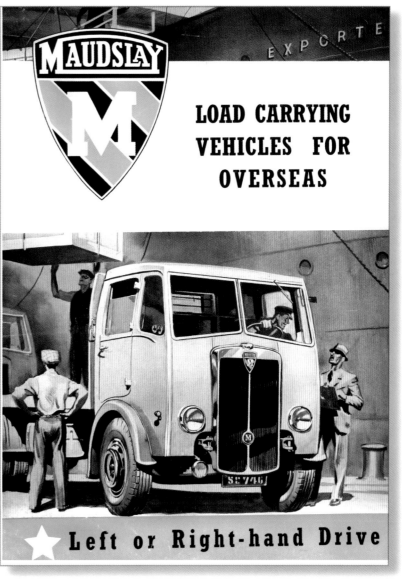

MAUDSLAY

LOAD CARRYING VEHICLES FOR OVERSEAS

Left or Right-hand Drive

Both Mustang and
Meritor had twin
steering.

The Mustang chassis had
a wheelbase of 18ft.

This Meritor's wheelbase was 17ft 6in. Smallest of the
Maudslay range was the Mogul, made in two sizes: the
Mogul II with 13ft 6in wheelbase and the Mogul III
with one of 16ft. All had vacuum servo hydraulic brakes.

GUE·343

By the early 1950s Maudslay was part of Associated Commercial Vehicles and real Maudslays became a thing of the past with the advent of the A suffixed range. Noticeable differences in this view of a Meritor Mk IIIA are the differing radiator shell and the lack of provision for a starting handle with 'M' escutcheon; the shunting jaws at the front of the chassis which were a feature of previous Maudslays are also gone. The Meritor now came on either a 14ft 6½in or 18ft 9½in wheelbase. Like the Maharajah it had air brakes and a choice of rear axles: double axle worm, or bevel drive and rigid or articulated bogie. Gross weights were 22 tons for the home market or 25½ tons for export.

The Maharanee Mk IIIA forward-control tractor chassis with 9ft 6in wheelbase. A bonneted version was also catalogued with a 12ft 1in wheelbase. It came with a 9.6-litre AEC diesel as standard but an 11.3-litre could be fitted as an alternative, except in conjunction with the lowest of the three rear-axle ratios available. Both were made with right- or left-hand drive and the gross permissible weight with trailer was 22 tons for home market models and 25 tons for export.

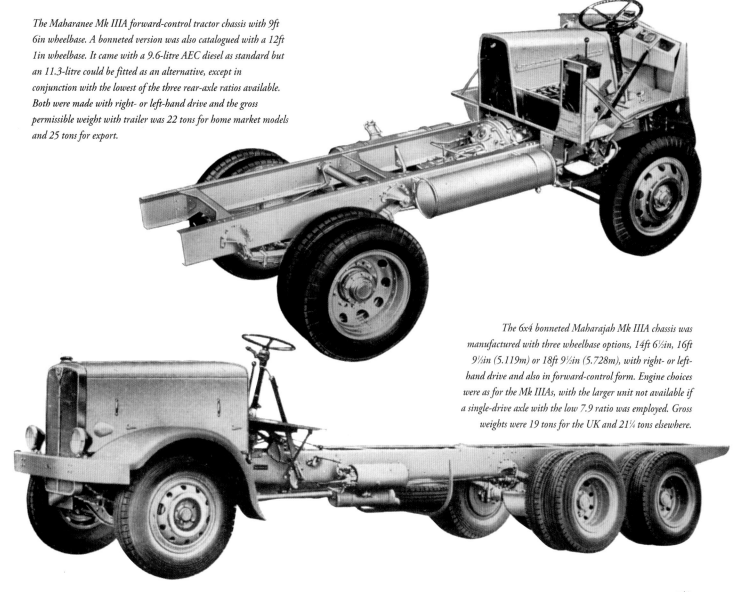

The 6x4 bonneted Maharajah Mk IIIA chassis was manufactured with three wheelbase options, 14ft 6½in, 16ft 9½in (5.119m) or 18ft 9½in (5.728m), with right- or left-hand drive and also in forward-control form. Engine choices were as for the Mk IIIAs, with the larger unit not available if a single-drive axle with the low 7.9 ratio was employed. Gross weights were 19 tons for the UK and 21¼ tons elsewhere.

MORRIS
COMMERCIAL

The car manufacturing company founded by William Morris in 1913 had grown in 10 years to become the largest in Great Britain and so, with funds available for further expansion, Morris decided to enlarge the scope of his empire to include commercial vehicles. Anxious that his existing factory at Cowley near Oxford should devote itself entirely to the manufacture of cars, he set about locating suitable premises for this new venture, but he did not have to look far. During his first few years as a manufacturer he had employed a number of outside suppliers and one of these, the Birmingham-based firm of E G Wrigley and Co, had supplied him with axles and

steering boxes. However, having lost its Morris contract some time before and then been let down by other customers, Wrigley was in dire financial straits and up for sale.

In 1923 Morris had acquired his engine supplier, Hotchkiss, which was based in Coventry. It made geographical sense to utilise Wrigley's nearby Birmingham premises, which were duly purchased. Morris moved in on the first day of January 1924 and incorporated his Morris Commercial Cars Ltd at the beginning of February. As a matter of interest, the Wrigley works was to remain William Morris's personal property until the latter part of 1936, when he sold it to Morris Motors.

The firm's first commercial, which utilised an almost identical version of the 1.8-litre engine and gearbox used in the Morris Oxford, was a 1-tonner available as either a lorry or van; at first sales were not encouraging, but within a year they had multiplied and Morris Commercials were on their way.

By 1926 a 30cwt Z-type lorry was catalogued and the firm was busy with experimental half-track versions of its 1-tonner as well as the 6x4 D type, with an eye to use by the services. For 1929 a six-wheeler which could carry 2½ tons was announced, and

With the war over only a couple of months previously, this November 1945 brochure was strictly utility: 'A tyre and tube can be supplied for the spare rim at extra cost'. With its 9ft 9in wheelbase and an overall length of just over 16ft it was a handy size, while 'Its economical 4 cylinder 2050cc ohv engine, shock absorbing clutch and long life third gear give it a performance second to none, and the ease with which it will thread its way through traffic make it an ideal driver's vehicle.'

THE WISE OPERATOR ALWAYS CHOOSES

Vehicles are only available against Ministry of War Transport Licences to Acquire

shortly afterwards the firm's first heavier truck in the form of the 5-ton Courier. Passenger vehicles in both single- and double-deck form had also been developed and were on the market by this time.

By 1932 the firm had outgrown its original premises and a move was made to a 17-acre site at Adderly Park, Birmingham. There, larger trucks up to 12 tons were designed and reached the experimental stage, but none went into production and it was the C range up to 3 tons and the Leader, which could carry up to 5 tons, that formed the bulk of the firm's output during the mid-1930s. In the years immediately preceding the war, two models, the PV 1-ton van and the larger Equiload, which were to last into the 1950s, were introduced, and then finally on the eve of hostilities a 5-ton forward-control truck.

The Nuffield Group, as William Morris's empire was now known, turned out almost every imaginable product, from gas masks to tanks and aeroplanes, in its many factories between 1939 and 1945. Vehicle production centred around the CDF 6x4, a development of the C model which had first seen the light of day back in 1926, and the 15cwt CS8. Both of these were adapted for a multitude of roles from Bofors gun platform to signals unit. Many thousands were made, as well as the much smaller PU cwt.

No real changes took place in the initial postwar range, which consisted of the LC, its larger lookalike the 2/3-tonner in lorry or van form, as well as forward-control and bonneted 5-tonners. By the beginning of the 1950s the only real additions had been the new 5-ton FVO forward-control truck as a replacement for the ageing model of the same type, along with a complimentary tipper and a tractor unit. There was also the LD2 van, but some of the other 'new' models were minimally rehashed versions of the firm's existing wares.

A merger was agreed during 1952 between the Nuffield Group and Austin, and two years later the name Morris-Commercial was done away with. In the ensuing years the British Motor Corporation, as the conglomerate was known, marketed the group's commercials as Austin, Morris or BMC. Thus, for instance, in 1955 what was termed the new Morris 2/3-tonner normal-control truck looked not unlike an Austin Loadstar with an elongated snout.

This harmless badge engineering continued right up to the late 1960s, when BMC was coerced into merging with Leyland by the government, and from then on the larger commercials were named Leyland. The light and medium vehicles were badged Austin-Morris, but even those disappeared some years ago and nowadays all we are left with are distantly related descendents with the anonymous title of LDV.

MORRIS-COMMERCIAL
5-ton
FORWARD CONTROL

- Powerful 4-cylinder engine developing 70 b.h.p.
- Sturdy transmission including 11 in. single plate clutch.
- Fully floating rear axle with straddle mounted pinion.
- Powerful Lockheed-Girling two-leading-shoe brakes with 16 in. dia. drums.
- Specially designed cam and roller steering gear.

Both forward- and normal-control 5-tonners had the same 13ft 6in wheelbase but the former had more generous inside body dimensions of 16ft 6in by 6ft 6in. Cabs were pressed steel and the standard dropside body was constructed of timber with a floor of tongued and grooved planks on a hardwood frame.

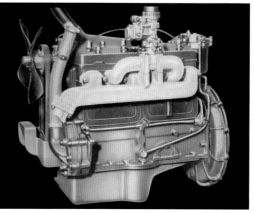

The company lauded their powerful engine but the 3519cc sidevalve four-cylinder produced just 20bhp per litre – low by today's standards but rather more than the diesels of that time could manage. Besides which the speed limit for this type of vehicle was just 30mph, allowing a low rear axle ratio of 7.57:1 in order to help things along a little.

This sales folder for the LC, with its naïve interpretation of both the vehicle and the uses it might be put to, served for several years from 1949 on.

The van version might have been hard to resist once one had absorbed some of the things that the makers had to say about it, including 'The driving seat is well positioned and all controls are easily operated, thus driving fatigue is virtually eliminated.'

By 1950 the new forward-control 5-tonner had come on the market. Tippers and tractors had a 9ft wheelbase, trucks 12ft 6in. The factory had managed to coax the old sidevalve petrol engine up to 80bhp, and a diesel was an alternative.

The driver's cab has been carefully designed for his comfort, safety and freedom from driving fatigue. The large cabin, wide-opening doors and low running-board make this cab as easy to enter or leave as a saloon car.

'The proved Morris-Commercial-Saurer diesel engine has many advantages to offer.' In fact the 4¼-litre 70bhp engine, of Saurer design but modified and built by Morris, probably didn't have any advantages; it was not a good motor.

The steel disc wheels are fitted with special extra low pressure ambulance tyres of large section

Although it shared the same 12ft 6in wheelbase as the forward-control truck some of its running gea,r the ambulance had a 4196cc six-cylinder ohv motor rated, conservatively I suspect, at 70bhp. The 1952 colour brochure offered various body styles from approved makers such as Stewart & Arden, but this photograph shows an earlier version from the 1950 brochure – 'A portable first-aid cabinet, water jug and glasses are standard equipment'.

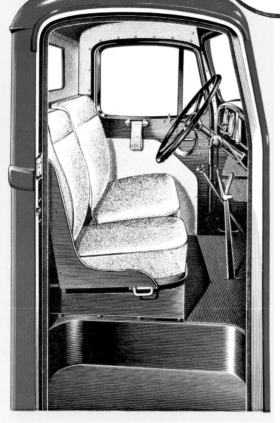

1 ▶ All-steel, double-skinned cab roof, with occupants insulated against heat or cold.

2 ▶ Wide bench-type seat for three. Driver's portion adjustable and upholstered in Dunlopillo.

3 ▶ Full-width doors—no cut-aways for wheel arch clearance.

4 ▶ Balanced windows.

5 ▶ Recessed interior door handles.

6 ▶ Car-type facia panel with document boxes either side.

7 ▶ Built-in step for extra safety.

8 ▶ Provision for heater, demister and radio.

9 ▶ Floor, free from obstructions, gives ample leg-room.

10 ▶ Cab interior finished in car style in brown and cream.

11 ▶ Cab doors lock.

12 ▶ Maximum all-round vision.

> *Here's the truck for me. It will save me time and money*

MORRIS-COMMERCIAL

New 1½ ton truck

> *With new all steel safety cab*

> *This is the truck for me with all the comfort and safety I want*

The LC4 was nothing more than old wine in an old bottle with a fresh label. The bespectacled gentleman's comment, if one sees him as Nuffield management rather than a customer, could be considered a little black humour!

1 ▶ Transverse bracing of the chassis frame ensures rigidity, prevents lozenging. **2** ▶ Side-members reinforced for extra strength. **3** ▶ Frame is of double thickness immediately behind the cab. **4** ▶ Two-piece propeller shaft with rubber-mounted centre bearing gives smooth transmission at all speeds. **5** ▶ Semi-elliptic springs front and rear (progressive type). **6** ▶ Steel disc wheels, five-stud fixing, with hub caps. **7** ▶ Four-speed gearbox with provision for power take-off. **8** ▶ Petrol tank capacity of 11 gallons. **9** ▶ Spare wheel housed under the chassis frame. **10** ▶ Rear axle with spiral bevel drive and four-star differential.

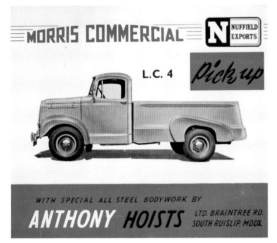

MORRIS COMMERCIAL **N** NUFFIELD EXPORTS

L.C. 4 *Pick up*

WITH SPECIAL ALL STEEL BODYWORK BY

ANTHONY HOISTS LTD. BRAINTREE RD. SOUTH RUISLIP, MDDX.

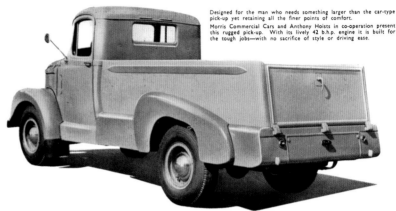

Designed for the man who needs something larger than the car-type pick-up yet retaining all the finer points of comfort.
Morris Commercial Cars and Anthony Hoists in co-operation present this rugged pick-up. With its lively 42 b.h.p. engine it is built for the tough jobs—with no sacrifice of style or driving ease.

Flush-fitting sliding doors, fitted on each side of the driver's cab, give freedom from draughts and prevent dust from entering the interior of the van.

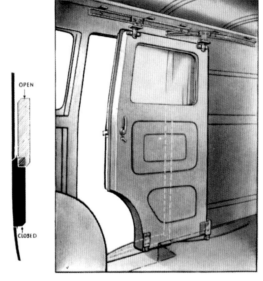

This rather unhappy vehicle (above) with pick-up body redolent of the lower half of a 1950s caravan was, so far as I am aware, sold exclusively abroad. Nuffield Exports' attempt to ape the fashionable American pick-ups of the time were less than successful..

The LD2 was at least a styling departure from what had gone befor,e but a lot of what lurked underneath, such as the trusty little 2050cc ohv engine, still producing its regulation 42bhp, was not so new.

MC-1952

The New MORRIS-COMMERCIAL

Series LD.2 1½ Ton Delivery Van

Designed to meet a world demand for a vehicle with medium van capacity.
Powered by a four-cylinder O.H.V. engine, the Series LD.2 1½ ton Delivery Van has a capacity of 235 cubic feet (6 6 cubic metres), from back of driver's compartment. The all-metal panelled body is attractively styled. Flush-fitting, draught excluding sliding doors on both sides of the driver's compartment enhance the appearance and add to its usefulness and safety. The wide-opening rear doors are hung on outrigger hinges and can be fastened in the fully opened position or folded flat against the sides of the van—an invaluable feature especially for loading and unloading against bays.

With Morris now a part of the British Motor Corporation, some puzzling external changes had taken place. The LD van had been given a new nose, the precursor of a style used for Morris Commercials from then on, but rather perversely the forward-control 5-ton trucks, instead of receiving the same treatment, had gained one uncannily like the type that had just departed from the LD. All 5-tonners, including the new short-wheelbase tractor unit, were given the option of a 4½-litre six cylinder petrol engine, and the prospect of a fresh diesel power plant was on the horizon.

The ageing 2/3-tonner, which was visually a slightly scaled-up version of the LC, now could be had with BMC's 3.4-litre four-cylinder diesel or its six-cylinder petrol engine as alternatives to the long-serving petrol four.

In my eyes Austin had often produced more aesthetic sales material than Morris, and certainly once Morris-Commercial had become part of BMC its brochures moved on from the plain dull and sometimes ham-fisted output of the previous 10 years or so. On this page we show the cover of a sumptuous and glossy showroom giveaway from August 1956, and on the next two pages some of its contents. All this leads me to the conclusion that the Austin advertising department had taken precedence in the merger.

The 5-ton normal-control long-wheelbase (13ft 4in) truck was available with BMC's 5.1-litre six-cylinder diesel and 4-litre six-cylinder petrol engines. The latter was the old Austin Princess unit, which also found its way into sporting vehicles such as the Jensen 541. The eagle-eyed amongst you will of course have noticed that this Morris bears an uncanny resemblance to contemporary Austin trucks, the Morris's extended nose coming off less well in the beauty stakes. With identical styling there was also a 4-tonner on the same wheelbase, but with a 3.4-litre four-cylinder diesel, and a 2/3-tonner with 11ft 6in wheelbase and either the 3.4 diesel or the 4-litre petrol engine.

All forward-controls now had unified frontal styling. Here is the short-wheelbase (7ft 1in) tractor which was fitted with either the 5.1-litre diesel or the 4-litre petrol engine. A gross train load of 12 tons was the norm, the optional Eaton two-speed axle increasing this to 15 tons.

The normal-control tractor had a 9ft 8½in wheelbase and the same engine and load specifications as the forward-control version.

This 7-ton forward-control was named the Morris BMC and had a 12ft 6in wheelbase. It was only produced with the 5.1-litre diesel but an Eaton two-speed axle and power steering were standard.

The BMC six-cylinder ohv diesel. With bore and stroke of 95 x 120mm giving a capacity of 5103cc it developed 105bhp at 2400rpm. It had a seven-bearing crankshaft and detachable wet liners.

Diesel engine manufacturers were forever coming out with fresh combustion chamber characteristics to aid efficiency, and here we see BMC's version – 'Shrouded inlet valves which produce a controlled air swirl in each cylinder'.

The forward-control was strictly a two-seater, whereas the normal-control boasted a cab which was supposed to be 'the widest in the British commercial vehicle industry'.

That was as may be, but it certainly looks pretty cramped with the two shop foremen and a curiously expressionless interloper from management ready for the road.

The Eaton two-speed axle was electrically operated on the 7-tonner and by vacuum on 5-tonners.

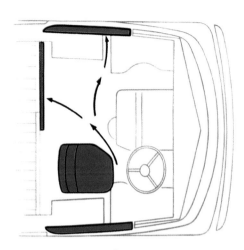

room to move

The vertical rear end of the engine cowling makes
it easy for the driver to get into the body of the
van or to get out on the left-hand-side.

MORRIS
2 TON DIESEL VAN
FORWARD CONTROL

350 cu. ft. Capacity!

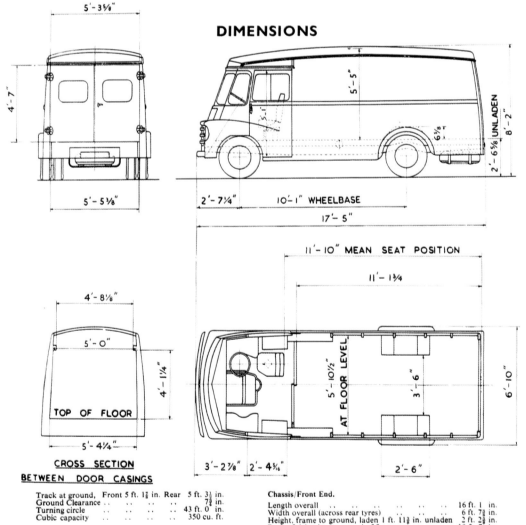

DIMENSIONS

5' - 3⅝"

4' - 7"

5' - 5⅛"

5' - 5"

8' - 2" UNLADEN

2' - 6⅜" UNLADEN

6⅜"

2' - 7¼"   10' - 1" WHEELBASE

17' - 5"

11' - 10" MEAN SEAT POSITION

11' - 1¾

4' - 8⅛"

5' - 0"

4' - 1¼"

TOP OF FLOOR

5' - 4¼"

**CROSS SECTION
BETWEEN DOOR CASINGS**

5' - 10½" AT FLOOR LEVEL

3' - 6"

6' - 10"

3' - 2⅞"   2' - 4⅝"

2' - 6"

Track at ground, Front 5 ft. 1¾ in. Rear 5 ft. 3¼ in.
Ground Clearance .. .. 7¾ in.
Turning circle .. .. 43 ft. 0 in.
Cubic capacity .. .. 350 cu. ft.

Chassis/Front End.

Length overall .. .. 16 ft. 1 in.
Width overall (across rear tyres) .. .. .. 6 ft. 7¾ in.
Height, frame to ground, laden 1 ft. 11⅜ in. unladen 2 ft. 2⅞ in.
Back of driver's seat to end of frame .. .. 10 ft. 7 in.
Back of driver's seat to centre rear axle .. 7 ft. 4 in.
Max. legal length behind driver's seat .. 12 ft. 4½ in.

*The 2-ton van is depicted in a
rather unlikely guise on the
cover of a May 1958 brochure:
the sliding racks containing the
bread would have had to be
about 11ft long to access the
stock from the rear.*

The 3.4-litre four-cylinder BMC diesel engine, which was by this time fitted into several of the group's commercials, developed 52bhp at 2500rpm.

What a charming period scene and, with 60 odd feet of floor space, what an ideal vehicle to use as a travelling library. However, by consulting the dimension chart on the previous page you will see that the lady librarian, complete with high-heeled shoes, stands only 4ft 7ins tall, so it would be outside browsing only for the gentleman unless he wanted to do it at a crouch.

you can take it anywhere!

The forward- and normal-control tractors, or prime movers, for 1960 had either the BMC 5.1-litre diesel engine or the 4-litre petrol six-cylinder. Wheelbase for the forward-control was 7ft 1in and for the normal-control 9ft 8½in. Maximum load was 12 tons, which was increased to 15 if the optional Eaton two-speed axle was fitted. During manufacture the rear of the chassis frame was left open, to be braced by a member to suit the trailer gear (eg Scammell or other) which was going to be used.

During 1961 a heavier tractor unit was introduced to the range.

Some minor restyling at the front had made the 3-tonner just a little less ungainly by 1960. Advertising still illustrated three-abreast seating and urged 'It is essential that your drivers should be comfortable'. The passengers here are apparently having an earnest discussion relating, perhaps, to the rather selfconscious looking-driver's apparent inability to put his shoes on the correct feet.

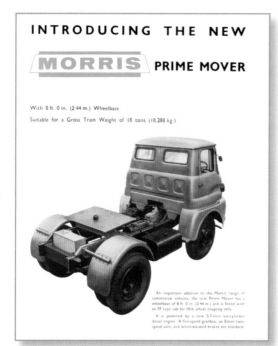

INTRODUCING THE NEW

MORRIS PRIME MOVER

With 8 ft. 0 in. (2·44 m.) Wheelbase

Suitable for a Gross Train Weight of 18 tons (18,288 kg.)

An important addition to the Morris range of commercial vehicles, the new Prime Mover has a wheelbase of 8 ft. 0 in. (2·44 m.) and is fitted with an FF type cab for fifth wheel coupling only.

It is powered by a new 5·7-litre six-cylinder diesel engine. A five-speed gearbox, an Eaton two-speed axle, and servo-assisted brakes are standard.

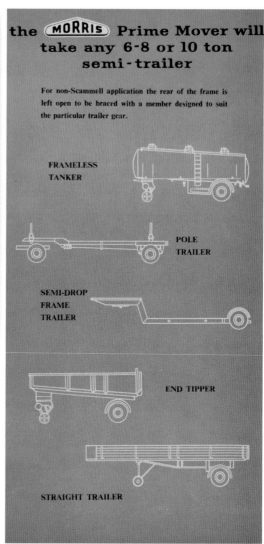

the **MORRIS** Prime Mover will take any 6-8 or 10 ton semi-trailer

For non-Scammell application the rear of the frame is left open to be braced with a member designed to suit the particular trailer gear.

FRAMELESS TANKER

POLE TRAILER

SEMI-DROP FRAME TRAILER

END TIPPER

STRAIGHT TRAILER

adaptable...

to a wide range...

of purposes...

FORSYTE FURNITURE CO. LTD. SWANSEA

GB OIL CO

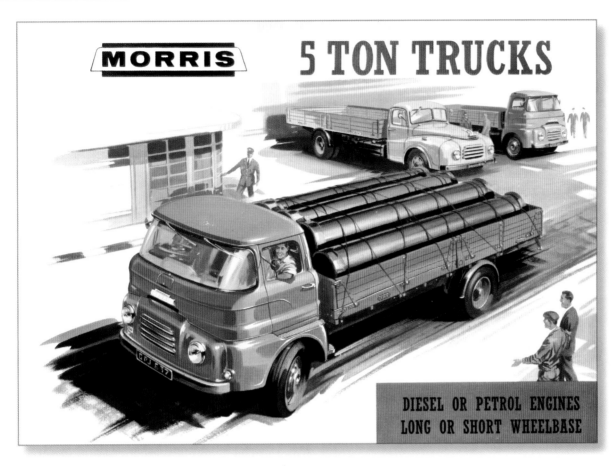

MORRIS **5 TON TRUCKS**

DIESEL OR PETROL ENGINES
LONG OR SHORT WHEELBASE

Here, the probable object was to show the company's modern forward-control trucks in the best light, but the artist has succeeded in making the poor old normal-control in the background more of an ugly duckling than ever. Both came on a 13ft 4in wheelbase and there was a short-wheelbase (10ft) Tipper version of the normal-control. All had the 5.1-litre diesel engine or the 4-litre petrol.

You got dual wipers chucked in for free with the forward-control but only one for the driver on the others – so much for three-abreast seating.

MORRIS

FF K140
7 TON FORWARD CONTROL TRUCKS

"pressed steel-tough-safe!"

Top of the truck range for 1962 was the FF 7-tonner. The brochure's emphasis on its steel cab – 'Built all in steel, it has the strength to take the knocks of heavy usage.' – could also be taken as a gibe against various other manufacturers who had gone over to glassfibre with its inflammable properties.

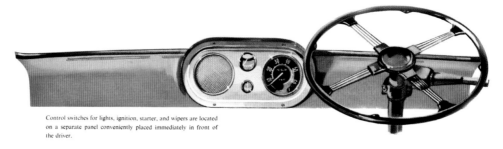

Control switches for lights, ignition, starter, and wipers are located on a separate panel conveniently placed immediately in front of the driver.

ENGINEERED FOR LONG LIFE AND TOUGH DUTY

Morris FF K140 trucks are *planned* for cross-country jobbing. Big value in first buy, they quickly pay dividends in lower operating costs. With either the B.M.C. 5·1-litre or 5·7-litre diesel engine for power, they hustle big loads tirelessly along trunk road and motorway.

Products of the vast technical resources of the British Motor Corporation Morris FF K140 trucks are available in a variety of specifications and with a choice of three wheelbases—10 ft. 0 in. (3·04 m.), 12 ft. 6 in. (3·81 m.), and 13 ft. 4 in. (4·06 m.).

"...and handsome too.!"

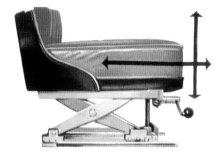

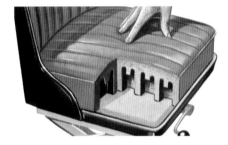

5.7 litres of BMC diesel, giving 105bhp at 2400rpm.

Here's what makes the miles flash by!

The range of what Morris called 'angle planned' trucks had become known as the FG series by 1962.

*The clever design of the cab
certainly did increased vision,
but whether the low quarter
glass panels really were 'a
valuable safety aid when
driving in fog' I would not like
to say. The doors actually
project far less (2 inches) than
the artwork would suggest,
which was a good safety factor,
but I would love to know how
they arrived at another of their
claims: 'Tests with the FG cab
prove that the driver's energy
expenditure is nearly three
times less than with the
conventional-type cab'.*

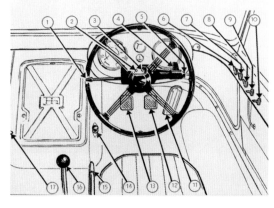

Controls and switches

1 Flashing indicator switch.	6 Panel lamp switch.	12 Brake pedal.
2 Flasher warning lamp.	7 Interior lamp switch.	13 Clutch pedal.
3 Main-beam warning lamp.	8 Windscreen wiper switch.	14 Stop control (diesel).
4 Main lighting switch.	9 Heater switch.	15 Brake hand lever.
5 Horn-push.	10 Heater switch.	16 Gear change lever.
	11 Accelerator pedal.	17 Choke control (petrol).

*The chassis frame was constructed of ⁵⁄₃₂in steel plate with 7½in deep
side members for the K30 and K40s, the plate thickness being
increased to ⁵⁄₁₆in for the K60 and K80s, while the K100s had ¼in
plate with 9⅛in deep side members.*

The FG30 was fitted with either the excellent BMC 4 cylinder 2.2-litre diesel or a petrol engine of the same capacity. Its wheelbase was of 9ft 6in as was the K40's unless the longer 10ft 9in was specified. In either event there was a choice of three engines for the K40: a 4-litre petrol and either 3.4- or 3.8-litre diesel. The same variety of engines applied to both K60 and K80, which had a common wheelbase of 12ft 1in. The K100 either had the 4-litre petrol motor or 5.1-litre diesel, and its wheelbase was 13ft 4in. The model numbers referred to capacity, hence a K30 could carry 30cwt/1½ tons and the K100 100cwt/5 tons.

The nose of the K100 protruded further than other K series and had air intakes of a different form.

SCAMMELL

The firm of Scammell Lorries Ltd was set up during 1922 in a new factory at Watford, north of London. Its origins, however, were in an East London motor repair and coachbuilding firm which, immediately after the First World War, had developed an articulated lorry.

From the outset Scammell specialised in this form of commercial vehicle. It was almost certainly the first firm in Britain to produce 'matched' six-wheelers in both flatbed and tanker form. By the mid-1920s the company was confident enough to increase the size of its largest artic to 15 tons as well as to introduce a six-wheeler tractor named the Pioneer which had excellent cross-country capabilities due to its novel rocking-beam rear axles and pivoting front axle. For 1928 Scammell brought out a conventional 6-ton four-wheeler truck and a year later had the distinction of producing a pair of what were most probably the world's largest lorries, artics having a capacity of nearly 100 tons.

Around this time the company began to experiment with various conversions to the Pioneer with an eye to military use, but it was to be a few years before anything of this nature was to become of paramount importance so, with sales suffering from the slump, Scammell cast around for gainful employment. Railway companies were keen to modernise their method of parcel delivery and to this end, in spite of already having been pre-empted by a competitor, the London & North Eastern Railway approached the former car manufacturer Napier for help. At this time Napier was almost exclusively an aero engine maker: it did some design and prototype work on the project but was more than happy to pass it on to Scammell for a fee. After evaluating Napier's experimental version, Scamell came up with its own interpretation during 1934: this was the quaint Scammell 'mechanical horse'. It consisted of an articulated unit with a single front wheel to the tractor and could be had, from the first, in either 3- or 6-ton versions.

With the economic situation improving as the 1930s progressed and its products enjoying a healthy export market, Scammell decided to branch out from their speciality and began to manufacture both six- and eight-wheeler rigid trucks.

Earlier work on militarising the Pioneer came to fruition in 1939 when war was declared and, for the next five years, the factory was fully employed producing versions of it as artillery tractors, tank transporters and other applications as well as all-terrain heavy vehicles.

The expertise that the company had accumulated in this field was not wasted, and after the war it began to manufacture all wheel drive four- and six-wheelers, the Mountaineer and the Explorer, as well as a specialist tractor for fairground operators named the Showtrac. In the meantime Scammell was also making its established range of artics, including a completely redesigned version of the old mechanical horse. Within a few years the firm had further enlarged its range with the Constructor series, which could be had from Junior to Super and either as a tractor or as a rigid. Large dump trucks also were manufactured on the Mountaineer chassis and later on the larger Constructor.

Leyland bought Scammell during 1955 but things were allowed to remain very much as they had been with little in the way of new products until 1960

From the sublime to the ridiculous, to coin a phrase. Not exactly, but with a range from a quaint little three-wheeled tractor to the mighty Super Constructor, Scammell certainly went to extremes.

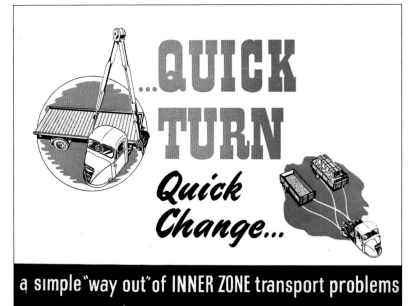

when the Routeman rigid eight-wheeler made its appearance, along with a forward-control tractor named the Handyman, both sharing the same cab design. The Routeman's cab was restyled a year later and the long-running Scarab given a shake up which resulted in a modernised version with four wheels known as the Scarab Four. The three-wheeler was given a futuristic fibreglass cab around 1966 and renamed the Townsman.

At the beginning of the 1970s Leyland began to exercise greater control. The firm became known as Scammell Motors and much of its development work resulted in an output which carried the Leyland badge. As Leyland's empire began its slide to disintegration Scammell had no means of escape, and the firm which for many years built some of the world's finest heavy haulage equipment finally ceased to exist in 1988.

The 'SCARAB' MECHANICAL HORSE

UNEQUALLED for operation in confined or crowded areas

In a world of traffic congestion the versatile "Scarab" Mechanical Horse is never in a tight corner. Its facility for getting in and out of confined spaces inaccessible to rigid vehicles reduces turn-round to an absolute minimum. The "Scarab" can couple instantly and automatically to a variety of trailers in turn, and no time is lost while the load is being handled.

In the present times of imperative economies the advantages of the Mechanical Horse are more than ever desirable.

FOR

INCREASED DELIVERIES	•	NO IDLE TRACTORS
NO LOADING DELAYS	•	LOW TAX
LOWER OPERATING COSTS		

THE most economical form of transport for short distance work.

SCAMMELL LORRIES LIMITED

The old mechanical horse reappeared after the war as the Scarab. Two versions were available, of 3- or 6-ton capability, propelled by a 2090cc four-cylinder sidevalve petrol engine. In later years four-cylinder Perkins diesel engines began to be fitted and, remarkably perhaps, the Scarab remained in production until 1967.

SCAMMELL 4, 6, 10 & 14 WHEEL PIONEER & CROSS COUNTRY VEHICLES

This range of vehicles was designed specifically for Pioneer operation over Virgin country, and can be supplied to withstand extreme climatic or altitude conditions. The ideal " go anywhere " vehicle for military purposes, prospecting, oilfields work, or for transporting heavy loads over soft or broken ground that would be impassable for the orthodox vehicle.

PIONEER 6 MOTIVE UNIT with Pole type semi-trailer for timber or pipe line tubes, 22,000 lb. direct pull winch. Load capacity 34,000 lbs.

MILITARY 14 TANK TRANSPORTER. Used by Fighting Services for recovery of disabled heavy Tanks, 22,000 lbs. direct pull winch. Load capacity 68,000 lbs.

PIONEER 6 PROSPECTOR can be supplied with 4 or 6 wheel drive. 22,000 lb. direct pull winch. Load capacity 15,000 lbs. and 26,000 lbs.

SCAMMELL SPECIALS

The Tractors, Machinery Transporters and Hoppers illustrated are but a small section of our range of special vehicles.

May we advise a type against your exact requirements ?

HIGHWAY HOPPER. Carries 27,000 lb. of road dressing. Selective compartments side dumping.

SHOWTRAC. For amusement caterers and travelling showmen. A 45,000 lb. tractor for hauling caravans, fitted with a 22,000 lb. dead pull winch and 35 KW Generator.

GRAIN HOPPER. Capacity 1,000 cubic ft. suitable for wheat, corn and similar seeds. Bottom discharge.

RIGID 8 with 2,200 Imp. Gals. tank for heavy Viscosity liquids. Discharged by air at 60 lbs. per square inch from Scammell 3 cylinder air compressor.

SCAMMELL RIGID EIGHT-WHEELERS

This range of vehicles is intended for operation over fairly good, hard ground, and can carry payloads up to 34,000 lbs., depending on tyre equipment fitted and condition of road surface. The standard machine has a single axle drive, but for more arduous conditions a double axle drive can be supplied.

RIGID 8 with 2,000 gals. Tar Spraying Tank. Tar heated electrically while travelling. Deposit automatically compensated for fluctuations of vehicle speed.

RIGID 8 with large capacity box body for light bulky loads.

ARTICULATED STRAIGHT 6 with hydraulically operated 735 cu. ft. end tipping body. Side tipping bodies can also be supplied.

SCAMMELL ARTICULATED 6 & 8 WHEELERS

The articulated range of vehicles will operate over bad, but fairly hard ground, and can carry a payload up to 25,000 lbs. for the " 6 " and 40,000 lbs. for the " 8," dependent on tyre equipment fitted, type of body, and condition of road or ground. Certain types of non-standard bodies are shown under "SPECIALS" below.

ARTICULATED STRAIGHT 6 with contractor's hinged-sided body.

ARTICULATED STRAIGHT 8 with flat platform body.

"Mountaineer" 19' Wheelbase "off the highway" Truck.
One of a number operating over virgin territory for the carriage of locust bait in Saudi Arabia.
130 b.h.p. engine provides ample power for trailer towing if necessary

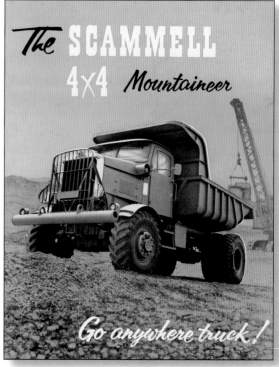

The **SCAMMELL** 4×4 *Mountaineer*

Go anywhere truck!

"Mountaineer" Articulated Timber Transporter 14' Wheelbase Motive Unit with 25 ton extensible Pole Trailer for forestry operation.

"Mountaineer" 17' Wheelbase Oilfields Motive Unit with bulk
cement hopper semi-trailer, load capacity 50,000 lbs.

FRAME. Sidemembers of sturdy channel section in carbon frame steel adequately braced by crossmembers.

ENGINE. Leyland 0/680 six-cylinder Diesel direct injection engine. Bore 127 mm. (5"). Stroke 146 mm. (5¾"). Cubic capacity 11.1 litres (677 cu. ins.). 150 B.H.P. at 2,000 R.P.M. governed speed. Compression ratio 15.75:1. Maximum torque 450 lb./ft. at 1,100 R.P.M.
ALTERNATIVELY IF SPECIFIED:
Rolls-Royce C6NFL. Bore 130 mm. (5⅛"). Stroke 152 mm. (6"). Cubic capacity 12.17 litres (743 cu. in.). 150 B.H.P. at 2,100 R.P.M. governed speed.
Scammell-Meadows 6.DC. 630. Bore 130 mm. (5⅛"). Stroke 130 mm. (5⅛"). Cubic capacity 10.35 litres (633 cu. in.). 125 B.H.P. at 1,750 R.P.M. governed speed.
Gardner 6LWK. Bore 107.95 mm. (4¼"). Stroke 152.4 mm. (6"). Cubic capacity 8.4 litres (511 cu. in.). 112 B.H.P. at 1,700 R.P.M. governed speed.

CLUTCH. 16" diameter. Single dry plate, with ball-bearing release bearing. Fully adjustable for wear. A clutch brake is operated by the clutch pedal and assists rapid upward gear changes.

GEARBOX. Six speeds under control of one lever working in visible gate. All gears except first and reverse are in constant mesh, with sliding dog engagement. Ball and roller bearings are used throughout. A gear type oil pump distributes a low viscosity oil round the box. The gearbox is mounted on rubber at three points and is thereby insulated from chassis distortion. A power-take-off capable of transmitting the full engine torque can be fitted. On the back of the gearbox is mounted the transposing drive for driving the front axle. The drive to the front axle is by means of a dog clutch operated from the driving seat as required (while the vehicle is in motion or stationary).

AVAILABLE WHEELBASES. 14' (168"); 17' (204"); 19' (228").

VEHICLE TYPES AVAILABLE	
a.	14' W.B. 8/10 cu. yard Dump Truck.
b.	14' or 17' W.B. Motive Unit with fifth wheel.
c.	14' W.B. Tractor for towing drawbar trailers.
d.	17' or 19' W.B. Oilfields Truck with special body.
e.	14', 17' or 19' W.B. Cross-country Load Carrier with body to suit specific requirements.

CROSS VEHICLE WEIGHT — 20 TONS 44,800 lbs.

GROSS TRAIN WEIGHT — 60 TONS 134,400 lbs.

POWER DRIVE FOR AUXILIARIES. A split transmission type of power take-off can be provided on the 17' and 19' W.B. models. The drive is taken to the front or rear and a choice of ratio varying from 1.5 step up, through 1 to 1, to 1.5 reduction is available. All gears including reverse can be utilised.
On the 14' W.B. model the power take-off is driven by means of a gear from the reverse idler in one direction only with main gear box in neutral. Suitable for intermittent duty at full engine torque.

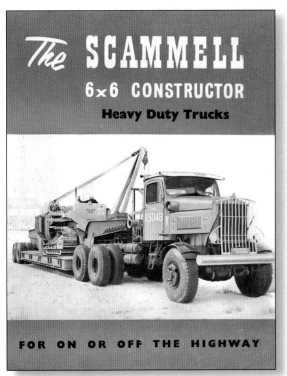

Scammell 21' 9" W B 6 x 6 Constructor Oilfields Bed Truck for 20 ton unitised loads.
See also 25' W B Super Constructor Oilfields Truck for loads up to 30 tons.

Scammell 15' 9" W/B 6 x 6 Constructor Oilfields Motive Unit with semi-trailer landing supplies for a desert oil rig.

FRAME. Sidemembers of deep Channel pressings with boxing plates in 12⅜"X4" Carbon Frame Steel adequately braced by cross-members.

ENGINE Rolls Royce C6NFL six-cylinder diesel direct injection. Bore 130 mm. (5⅛"). Stroke 152 mm. (6"). Cubic capacity 12.17 litres (743 cu. ins.). 185 B.H.P. at 2,100 R.P.M. governed speed.

Compression ratio 16:1. Maximum torque 505 lbs./ft.
Leyland 0.900 six-cylinder Diesel direct injection. Bore 140 mm. (5½"). Stroke 165 mm. (6½"). Cubic capacity 15.2 litres (927 cu ins.) 170 B.H.P. at 1,800 R.P.M. governed speed. Compression ratio 15:1. Maximum torque 550 lbs./ft. at 900/1,100 R.P.M.

CLUTCH. 18" diameter. Single dry plate with ball bearing release bearing. Fully adjustable for wear. A clutch brake is operated by the clutch pedal and assists rapid upward gear changes.

GEARBOX. Scammell six speed controlled by one lever working in visible gate. All gears except first and reverse are in constant mesh with sliding dog engagement. Ball and roller bearings are used throughout. A gear type oil pump distributes a low viscosity oil round the box. The gearbox is mounted on rubber at three points and is thereby insulated from chassis distortion. On the back of the gearbox is mounted a transposing box with separate output flanges for propellor shaft connection to each of the three axles. The transposing box incorporates an auxiliary two speed gearbox and a dog clutch for disengaging the drive to the front axle. Both are controlled by separate levers in the cab and can be operated with the vehicle in motion or stationary. A power-take-off capable of transmitting the full engine torque is available.

Gearbox ratios: 1, 6.55:1; 2, 4.07:1; 3, 2.53:1; 4, 1.61:1; 5, 1:1; 6, .622:1; R, 8.37:1; 2 speed auxiliary gearbox ratios. High 1,323:1; low, 2.535:1; Providing 12 forward and 2 reverse speeds.

AVAILABLE WHEELBASES 15' 9" (189"); 17' 8" (212"); 21' 9" (261"); 25' 1¾" (301¾").

VEHICLE TYPES AVAILABLE.
a. 15' 9" W/B heavy Duty Tractor for towing Drawbar Trailers.
b. 15' 9" or 17' 8" W/B Motive Unit with fifth wheel.
c. 15' 9" W/B Chassis for Mobile Cranes, Excavators etc.
d. 17' 8" or 21' 9" W/B Chassis for Mobile Well Servicing Hoists.
e. 21' 9" or 25' W/B Oilfields Bed Trucks.

GROSS VEHICLE WEIGHT (25' W/B) 46½ TONS.

DESIGNED WITH EXCEPTIONAL BOGIE ARTICULATION FOR CROSS COUNTRY WORK

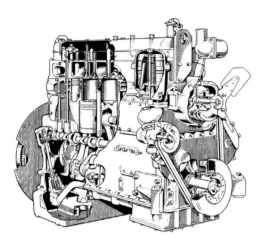

The Leyland "900" six-cylinder diesel engine fitted in the Super Constructor develops 230 B.H.P. at 1,900 r.p.m.

Bore 5·5 in. (139·7 mm.).   Stroke 6·5 in. (165·1 mm.).
Cubic capacity 926 cu. in. (15·2 litres).
Maximum torque 704 lb./ft. at 1,400 r.p.m.
Governed maximum speed 1,900 r.p.m.
As an alternative to above the Rolls-Royce C6.S 250 b.h.p. supercharged six-cylinder diesel engine can be supplied.

**The Self-changing
R.V. 30 Gearbox**
provides 8 speeds forward
and 2 reverse and in combination
with the "Fluidrive" stepped coupling
provides a highly efficient transmission
combining flexibility with ease of control.   A single speed transposing case
bolted to the rear provides output flanges for the three propeller shafts
and a power take-off transmitting full power in any of the gearbox ratios.

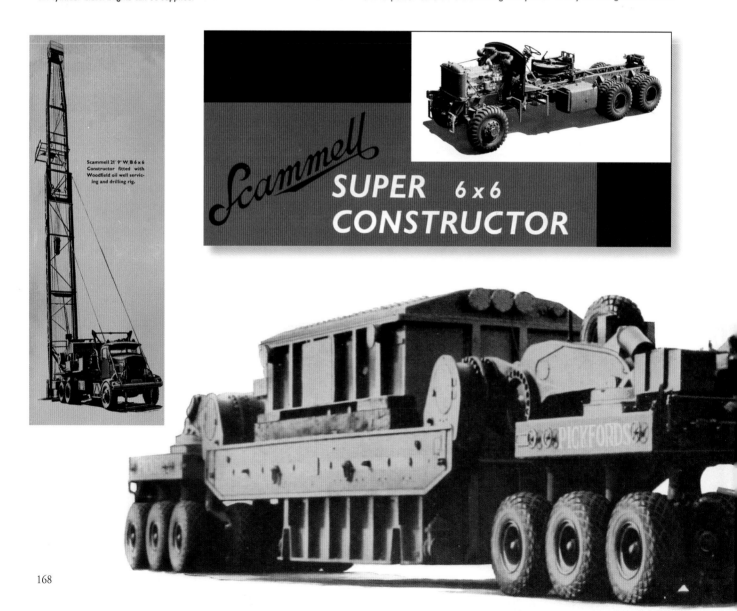

Scammell 21' 9" W.B 6 x 6 Constructor fitted with Woodfield oil well servicing and drilling rig.

Scammell SUPER 6 x 6 CONSTRUCTOR

"HIGHWAYMAN"

4 x 2 Motive Unit

This motive unit has been specially designed as a prime mover for use with Scammell semi-trailers. Together they form a completely matched articulated vehicle suitable for carrying general merchandise, liquids, solids in bulk and gases.

Gross Rating (Great Britain): 24 tons

By the end of the 1950s the 10ft wheelbase Highwayman series was as complex as other Scammells due to the firm's almost endless options list, devised to suit the multitude of tasks that the vehicles were called upon to perform. The 24-ton version had the option of three engines: the 11.1-litre Leyland 680, the 9.8-litre Leyland 600 or a Gardner 6LW of 8.4 litres. The largest, which was rated at 42 tons as a motive unit or 52 tons as a tractor and drawbar trailer, had either the Leyland 680 or a Gardner 6LX of 10.45 litres.

Scammell 15' 9" W B Heavy Duty Tractor hauling a Transformer, the gross train weight exceeding 200 tons.

One of the stars of the 1960 Commercial Motor Show was Scammell's brand new 'matched' artic, which was unveiled as being the last word in modern commercial vehicle design. It was fitted with a horizontal-type Gardner 6LX engine mounted behind the cab, mid-wheelbase and low down, in unit with Scammells' own six-speed gearbox. The driven bogie's suspension was by Hendrickson rubber cushions and the twin axles had epicyclic reduction gears in the hubs in addition to spiral bevel differentials. There were air-assisted hydraulic twin leading shoe brakes on all 10 wheels and the twin-cylinder compressor for these also supplied the semi-trailer with air for its brakes and for its air suspension if fitted. The quoted top speed was 42mph. Very few of this first type were made but it was reintroduced a few years later with a twin-steer 6x2 wheel plan.

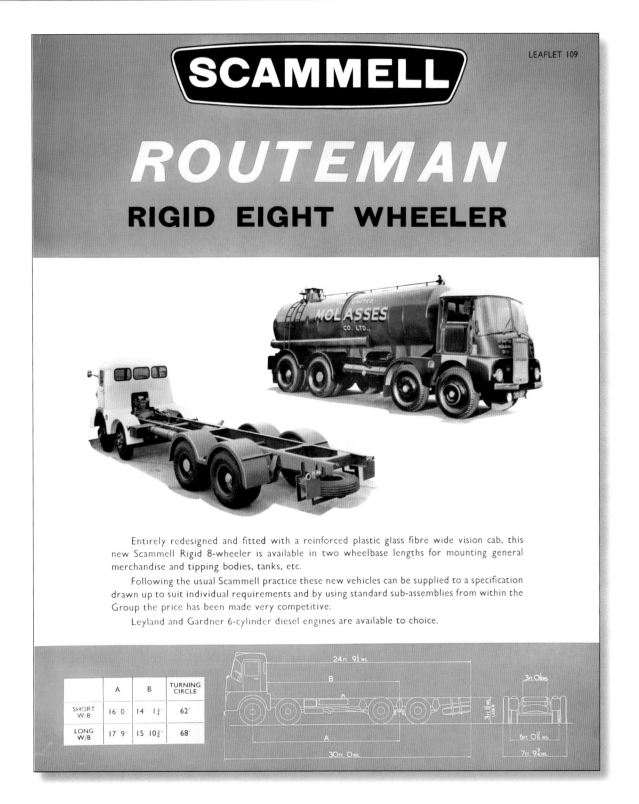

SCAMMELL

LEAFLET 109

ROUTEMAN
RIGID EIGHT WHEELER

Entirely redesigned and fitted with a reinforced plastic glass fibre wide vision cab, this new Scammell Rigid 8-wheeler is available in two wheelbase lengths for mounting general merchandise and tipping bodies, tanks, etc.

Following the usual Scammell practice these new vehicles can be supplied to a specification drawn up to suit individual requirements and by using standard sub-assemblies from within the Group the price has been made very competitive.

Leyland and Gardner 6-cylinder diesel engines are available to choice.

	A	B	TURNING CIRCLE
SHORT W/B	16 0"	14 1½"	62'
LONG W/B	17 9"	15 10¾"	68'

Scammell went into the early 1960s with this rigid eight-wheeler. As usual there was a range of specifications, including four engine options: the Leyland 600 and 680, and the Gardner 6LW and 6LX. The Scammell six-speed gearbox had a power take-off capable of transmitting full engine torque, an unusual fitment for a vehicle of this type, and the rear bogie could either have a single or twin driven axles.

SEDDON

Just before World War II the firm of Foster & Seddon of Lancashire, contractors and dealers in commercial vehicles, brought out a 6-ton lorry of its own make. Although nipped in the bud, so to speak, when the company was given contracts contributing to the war effort for the duration, this was not to mean the demise of the emergent marque.

Once the war was over production recommenced. In 1947 the company became Seddon Lorries Ltd and a move was made to nearby Oldham.

In 1950 a smaller 3-tonner was announced and in the same year there was another name change, to Seddon Diesel Vehicles Ltd. In contrast to some of the old established lorry manufacturers who were finding postwar conditions tough (and in some cases accepting takeover bids to keep their doors open) the youthful Seddon firm appeared to be flourishing. During the next few years it developed a mid-engined passenger chassis as well as a light 25cwt commercia,l and it was among the first firms to use moulded glassfibre for cab construction. In 1957 Seddon put its first heavyweight, a 24-tonner, into production and for export only introduced a 6x4 tractor which could haul 40 tons. These were by no means their only fresh models of the later 1950s, however: alongside a new passenger chassis were several capacities of truck with varying wheel configurations, culminating, size wise, in 1961 with a bonneted articulated truck rated at 45 tons.

A completely new series was brought on to the market in 1964 in the form of the 13:Four which was joined a year later by the larger 16:Four, both having engines supplied by Perkins, which had remained Seddon's preferred make since before the war.

The rival firm of Atkinson was taken over in 1970 by what was from now on known as Seddon Motors Ltd, but for the time being both companies continued to turn out their own products as though nothing had taken place.

With a totally new range of promising-looking heavy goods vehicles under development, Seddon fell prey to a takeover when it became the property of International Harvester during 1974. The following year, when the new heavies went on the market as the 400 Series, it had become Seddon-Atkinson Vehicles Ltd. Since 1992 International Harvester and therefore the Seddon-Atkinson brand have been owned by IVECO.

9' 0" WHEELBASE TRACTOR CHASSIS

Illustrated is an 8 Ton "Close coupled six wheeler," one of the many types of trailer to which this chassis is adaptable. Other types include articulated bus-bodies, large capacity removal vans, travelling store vans, etc.

Technical data :—Approximate turning circle of 34 feet dia. ; Perkins P.6 Mark 3N Diesel engine, developing 70 B.H.P (Max) Chassis weight (including cab) 5,600 lbs. ; Gearbox, I reverse and 4 forward gears ; 2 Speed Axle.

2-SPEED AXLE

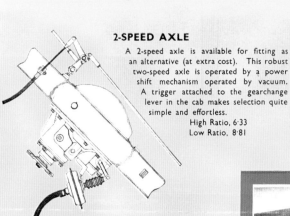

A 2-speed axle is available for fitting as an alternative (at extra cost). This robust two-speed axle is operated by a power shift mechanism operated by vacuum. A trigger attached to the gearchange lever in the cab makes selection quite simple and effortless.

High Ratio, 6·33
Low Ratio, 8·81

4-SPEED GEARBOX AND 2-SPEED AXLE

Gearbox Ratios		Overall		Tractive Effort	Road Speed	
		High	Low			
1st	5·27		46·42	5785	5·0	M.P.H.
		33·35		4160	6·95	,,
2nd	2·61		22·99	2868	10·08	,,
		16·52		2060	14·02	,,
3rd	1·70		14·97	1867	15·45	,,
		10·76		1342	21·50	,,
4th	Direct		8·81	1098	26·30	,,
		6·33		790	36·60	,,
Rev.	8·23		72·50	9040	3·20	,,
		52·09		6498	4·45	,,

The 1948 catalogue specified a two-speed axle for the Mk 5 tractor only. Seddon radiator shells of this period were cast aluminium. Brakes were twin leading shoe hydraulics by Lockheed with Clayton Dewandre vacuum servo assistance.

The fitting of this axle cuts down operational costs as well as reducing wear on the engine and transmission. It gives eight forward speeds and two reverse, permitting high speed for economy on long runs and an extra low gear for ascending the steepest gradients.

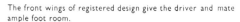

The front wings of registered design give the driver and mate ample foot room.

All vehicles are available left or right hand drive, with or without cab and or body.

Note the "Ki-Gass" starting equipment and "Perkins Starter-heater" for easy starting in cold weather (Right of steering column).

TIPPER

10' 0" WHEELBASE CHASSIS.
Standard 5½ cubic yard body,
equipped with "Pilot" power-
operated hydraulic-end tipping
gear, Model U.G.C/2, tipping angle
of up to 50 degrees. Three-way
tipping gear can be fitted alternatively if required.
4-speed gearbox
fitted with power
take-off pump.

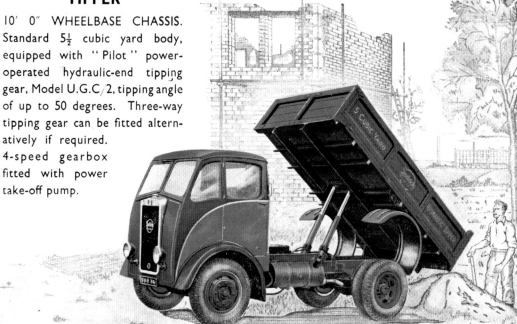

The Mk 5S tipper with the Mk
5L truck below. The truck had
a 13ft 6in wheelbase and was
fitted with a five-speed gearbox
which had an overdrive top
gear of 0.818 to 1. Both, along
with the tractor, had the
Perkins P6 Mk 3N six-cylinder
diesel of 4.73 litres, developing
70bhp at 2400rpm

The Perkins P6 being lowered into a chassis.

Cabs were still constructed with wooden framework to support the panels.

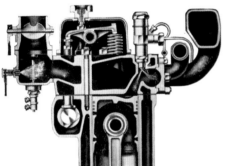

Cylinder head and "Aeroflow" combustion chamber

The Chassis . . .

The chassis is sturdily built with frame of deep channel section braced with generous cross members. At the same time by taking extreme care to reduce unladen weight to a minimum a perfect combination of lightness and strength has been achieved.

By 1950 the Perkins P6 engine, although of the same capacity, was producing 79bhp at 2400rpm. Engine manufacturers had differing thoughts on how to produce the most efficient combustion: this shows the Perkins method.

Wheelbase for tractors, tippers and the truck, shown here, remained the same. Headlamps were now recessed.

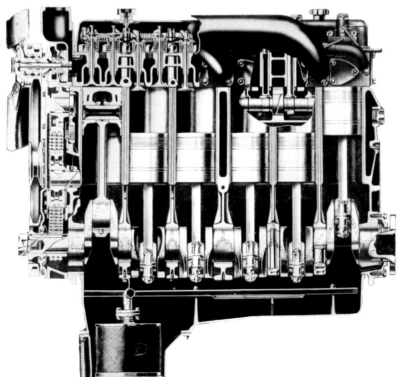

MK.5 GOODS VEHICLE
6-7 TON PAYLOAD

The Mk. 5L with R.H. or L.H. drive can be supplied as chassis only, chassis and cab, or complete with flat platform body, dropside or any special body to meet your particular requirements.

If desired a two-speed axle can be fitted as an alternative to the standard rear axle.

MK.5S10 TIPPER
6-7 TON PAYLOAD

The Mk. 5S10 tipper has a wheelbase of 10ft., and has the same high quality components as the 6 ton truck. "Pilot" power operated hydraulic end tipping gear is fitted. If desired 3-way tipping gear or a two speed axle can be fitted as alternatives to the standard equipment.

MK.5S9/2 TRACTOR
8-10 TON PAYLOAD

The Mk. 5S9 2 tractor as illustrated is shown with a "Carrimore" low loading trailer. This is one of the many types of trailer to which this chassis is adaptable. Other types include articulated bus bodies, large capacity removal vans, travelling store vans, etc.

Gardner diesel engines were also used in four-, five- or six-cylinder form (4LW, 5LW or 6LW). This is the five-cylinder unit.

Complete Range of
Seddon Diesels FOR LOADS UP TO 16 TONS

Seddon claimed to be pioneers in the use of glassfibre for cabs and at this time theirs featured translucent roofs.

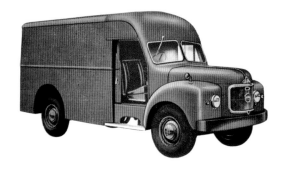

The 25/30cwt van with 10ft 1½in wheelbase, powered by a Perkins P3-144.

The Mk 7 3-tonner came as a van, truck, tipper or tractor on the following wheelbases: 10ft 6in, 8ft 9in or 6ft 10in. The Perkins P6 was available as an extra for the tractor only.

The 6/7-ton Mk 5 had been given a facelift but wheelbase options remained the same. Engines were either the Perkins P6 R2, which gave 104bhp, or the Gardner 4LK.

The Mk 16 5-tonner. Whether on an 11ft 6½in wheelbase in van or truck form, or as a flatbed with 15ft 6in wheelbase, all were powered by the Perkins P6, which now gave 83bhp.

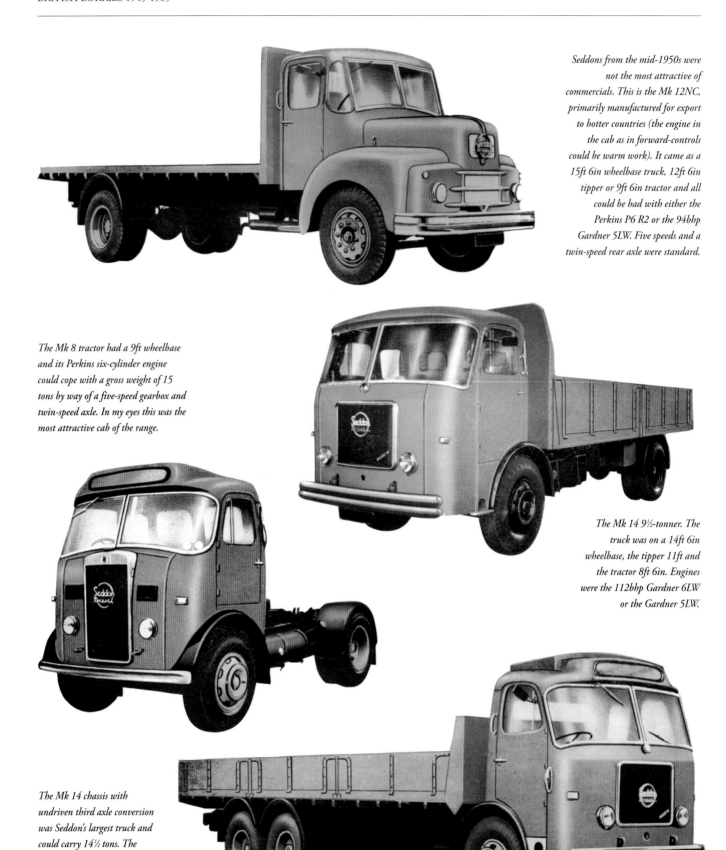

Seddons from the mid-1950s were not the most attractive of commercials. This is the Mk 12NC, primarily manufactured for export to hotter countries (the engine in the cab as in forward-controls could be warm work). It came as a 15ft 6in wheelbase truck, 12ft 6in tipper or 9ft 6in tractor and all could be had with either the Perkins P6 R2 or the 94bhp Gardner 5LW. Five speeds and a twin-speed rear axle were standard.

The Mk 8 tractor had a 9ft wheelbase and its Perkins six-cylinder engine could cope with a gross weight of 15 tons by way of a five-speed gearbox and twin-speed axle. In my eyes this was the most attractive cab of the range.

The Mk 14 9½-tonner. The truck was on a 14ft 6in wheelbase, the tipper 11ft and the tractor 8ft 6in. Engines were the 112bhp Gardner 6LW or the Gardner 5LW.

The Mk 14 chassis with undriven third axle conversion was Seddon's largest truck and could carry 14½ tons. The wheelbase was 16ft 8½in and it was powered by a Gardner 5LW or a 6LW.

SENTINEL

The Scottish firm of Alley & McLellan, whose Sentinel Engineering Works had been established in 1875 had, amongst other things, made something of a speciality of the manufacture of prefabricated ships for export in kit form. Conscious of the growing need for forms of land-borne commercial transport it began in around 1907 to produce a steam lorry named the Sentinel. This proved to have a ready market but by 1917 lack of space and industrial disputes prompted the factory to relocate south of the border.

With this move to Shrewsbury in Shropshire (and a renaming to The Sentinel Wagon Works Ltd) the company continued producing very much the same vehicles as before. A financial hiccup during 1920 necessitated some refinancing and the year of this reconstruction was inserted into the company name.

The 1947 Sentinel 7-ton tipper had an all-steel cab with an unusual feature which was unique to the firm's commercials: sliding doors. The wheelbase was a generous 12ft 8in, brakes were Lockheed hydraulic servo-assisted and the underslung Sentinel four-cylinder diesel engine of just over 6 litres, giving 90bhp at 2000rpm, was coupled to a four-speed gearbox.

This appeared to do the trick and during the remainder of the decade Setninel concentrated on refining its steam engines as well as bringing out its first six-wheeler in 1927 and an eight-wheeler in 1929. This vehicle can lay claim to being the first rigid eight-wheeler put into production. It was designed to get around the Construction and Use Regulations appertaining at that time, which restricted the load that a commercial vehicle could carry, depending on the number of its axles. The regulations allowed a two-axle lorry to have a maximum weight of 12 tons and a three-axle 19 tons; these could only be exceeded by using a tractor and trailer combination. Although the running costs of steam lorries were at this time still competitive with other fuels, the heavier weight of their machinery limited their carrying capacity compared with vehicles powered by internal combustion engines. Sentinel's eight-wheeler went a long way to redress the balance by having a 14-ton load capacity.

The early 1930s saw the firm going over to the use of pneumatic tyres and in 1934 it launched what was the last word, almost literally, in steam lorries, the S type with four-cylinder engine. Despite offering the S type in a choice of four-, six- or eight-wheelers, sales were not encouraging, and two years later the company was forced to refinance, emerging from this

with the title Sentinel Wagon Works (1936) Ltd.

In the years leading up to World War II Sentinel continued making improvements to the S series trucks but, during the war, when the factory was busy with government contracts, it at last dawned on the management that the days of the steam lorry really were unlikely to return and they began to make provisions for a switch to conventional propulsion.

In 1945 these preparations came to fruition when the firm put a petrol-engined truck into production, followed the following year by a 7/8-ton diesel version. Within two years the range grew to comprise rigids, tippers, tractors and even a chassisless bus with an under-floor engine.

Sentinel's steam lorries had their last hurrah in 1950 with a final export order of 100. As though to shrug off the last connection with steam, the company had for a while been known as Sentinel (Shrewsbury) Ltd.

Modernisation of the existing range and one or two fresh models kept Sentinel busy, but it was becoming increasingly difficult to make headway against larger competitors. Besides this, the company was becoming increasingly involved in railway contracts, which before long led it to cease lorry manufacture and dispose of redundant stock to Transport Vehicles Ltd in neighbouring Cheshire.

The 4/4 DV had a choice of either a 13ft 6in or 14ft 9in wheelbase in truck form and 12ft 8in as a tipper. Sentinel's four-cylinder diesel was now down rated to 80bhp at 1800rpm but the gearbox had acquired a fifth speed and brakes were Clayton Dewandre air-assisted. An old-fashioned touch was the trapdoor roof ventilator, another Sentinel hallmark.

APPROXIMATE LEADING DIMENSIONS

Wheelbase	..	..	..	..	..	15' 9"
Body length outside	..	..	..	..	..	22' 0"
Track at ground (Front)	..	..	..	..	6' 4⅜"
(Rear)						5' 8"
Overall length with body	..	..	..	..	27' 3"
,, width ..	..	..	..	..		7' 4"
,, height	..	..	..	..		7' 11¼"
Frame height laden	..	..	..	..		3' 1"
Turning Circle ..	..	..	..	..		59' 0"
Approx. unladen weight with flat platform body ..						5 t. 9 cwt.

Road speed in m.p.h. at 1,800 r.p.m. engine speed.

	5th	4th	3rd	2nd	1st	Rev.
R.A. Ratio 8¼ to 1 ..	32.6	24.4	13.6	7.55	4.0	4.08

The 4/6 DV came with identical mechanical specifications to the 4/4 DV apart from the rear bogie, which had a single overhead worm driven front axle with trailing rear axle.

Sentinel six cylinder four wheeler trailer model

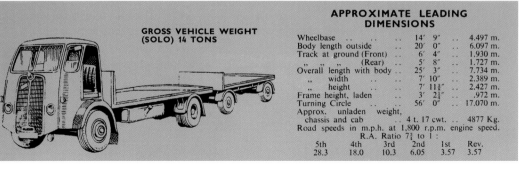

The DVE was the export version of the 6/4 and had a 9.12-litre six-cylinder version, with identical 121.05 x 133.35mm bore and stroke, of the Sentinel four-cylinder diesel. Brake horsepower was 120 at 1800rpm.

GROSS VEHICLE WEIGHT
(SOLO) 14 TONS

APPROXIMATE LEADING DIMENSIONS

Wheelbase	14′ 9″ ..	4.497 m.
Body length outside ..	20′ 0″ ..	6.097 m.
Track at ground (Front) ..	6′ 4″ ..	1.930 m.
,, ,, (Rear) ..	5′ 8″ ..	1.727 m.
Overall length with body ..	25′ 3″ ..	7.734 m.
,, width ..	7′ 10″ ..	2.389 m.
,, height ..	7′ 11⅜″ ..	2.427 m.
Frame height, laden ..	3′ 2¼″ ..	.972 m.
Turning Circle	56′ 0″ ..	17.070 m.

Approx. unladen weight,
chassis and cab .. .. 4 t. 17 cwt. .. 4877 Kg.
Road speeds in m.p.h. at 1,800 r.p.m. engine speed.
R.A. Ratio 7¾ to 1 :

5th	4th	3rd	2nd	1st	Rev.
28.3	18.0	10.3	6.05	3.57	3.57

The 6/6 DV had a 17ft 5½ in wheelbase and was powered by Sentinel's 9.12-litre diesel coupled to a five-speed gearbox. The rear bogie had a pair of identical overhead worm drive rear axles with a third differential incorporated in the leading axle. Air brakes were by Clayton Dewandre and maximum payload was 12 tons. Top speed was just 29.8mph at the engine's 1800rpm maximum.

THORNYCROFT

The first batch of Mighty Antar tractors was shipped to the Middle East for the Iraq Petroleum Company during 1950 to be used for the transport and stringing of pipe. The pipeline ran from Kirkuk to the port of Banias on the Eastern Mediterranean coast. The pipes handled weighed nearly 7 tons each and were 93 feet in length.

Having for some years been a builder of the then-fashionable steam launches which abounded on the River Thames, the firm of John I Thornycroft, located in Chiswick, decided to diversify operations to include steam-driven commercial vehicles. To this end a front wheel drive, rear-steering van was built which was exhibited at the Crystal Palace Motor Show in 1896.

Orders were taken and within two years, in order to gain more space, the company moved down to Basingstoke in Hampshire, where it constructed a vehicle which was almost certainly the first articulated lorry to be made in Britain. In the early years of the 20th century Thornycroft was beginning to enjoy a lucrative export market for its steam wagons and was also conducting trials with a steam-driven double-deck bus. However, unlike some other manufacturers of steam-driven commercials, Thornycroft did not see steam as the way forward, and by 1910 had all but abandoned it in favour of the internal combustion engine. By the outbreak of World War I it was offering a workmanlike range of petrol-engined trucks from 30cwt to 4 tons including a 3-ton subsidy model, the J type, which formed a part of the firm's government supply contracts for the following four years. It was Thornycroft's boat-building business, however, now

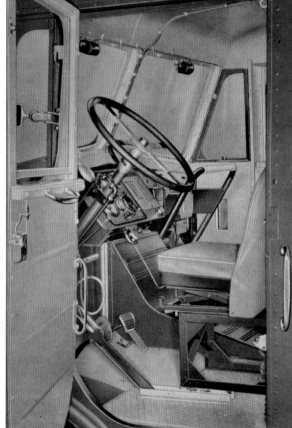

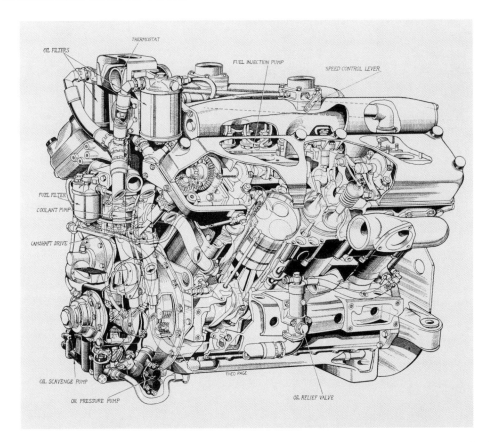

OIL FILTERS
THERMOSTAT
FUEL INJECTION PUMP
SPEED CONTROL LEVER
FUEL FILTER
COOLANT PUMP
CAMSHAFT DRIVE
OIL SCAVENGE PUMP
OIL PRESSURE PUMP
THEO PAGE
OIL RELIEF VALVE

The giant Rover Meteorite Mk 101 engine had a bore and stroke of 137 x 152.4mm and displaced 18 litres. It was a V8 diesel of interesting specification, with aluminium crankcase, cylinder block and heads, and bevel-driven overhead camshafts actuating one exhaust and two inlet valves per cylinder. Its power output was 250bhp at 2000rpm.

Dimensions shown on the plan below are in inches.

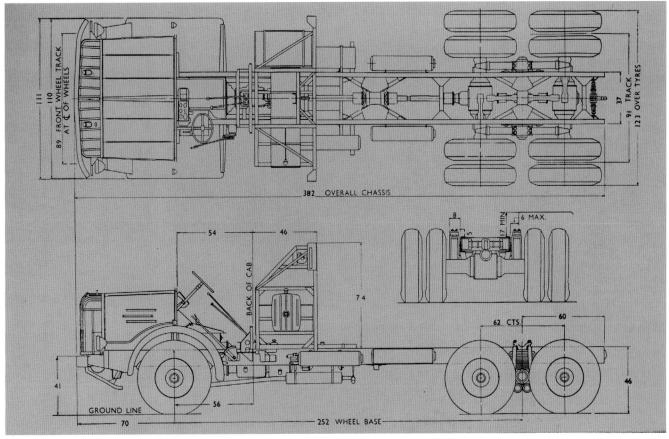

111
110
89 FRONT WHEEL TRACK AT ℄ OF WHEELS
37
91 TRACK
123 OVER TYRES
382 OVERALL CHASSIS
54
46
BACK OF CAB
74
8
17 MIN
6 MAX.
5
62 CTS
60
41
56
46
GROUND LINE
70
252 WHEEL BASE

Clutch and gearboxes assembly (there were two – a four-speed and an auxiliary three-speed with high, direct and low) along with dynamo, starters, compressor and clutch cooling fan.

Everything about the Antar was massively constructed and a great deal of thought was put into every detail of its design. For instance, the air for the twin-cylinder gearbox-driven compressor, after being drawn through the left-hand engine air cleaner, was passed through an anti-freezer to lower the freezing point of any airborne moisture - all in order to avoid any possibility of ice formation which might choke the air valves. The like of splendid leviathans such as the Antar will not be seen again.

Behind the twin radiators, the right-hand of which had a large oil radiator mounted in front of it, was this pair of cooling fans, which would look more at home on an aircraft than on a giant truck.

grown out of all proportion to its river launch days and relocated at Southampton, which took the lion's share, producing over 25 destroyers and three submarines during the war.

As other commercial vehicle manufacturers found, the end of the war did not signal an instant ready market for their wares due to the huge number of war-surplus trucks that could be had for very advantageous prices. Despite these conditions Thornycroft soon had trucks of between 2 and 6 tons on sale and by the early 1920s was making several passenger vehicle types. Throughout the years leading to the slump the variety of its products increased, demonstrating also some original thinking such as unit-construction engine and gearbox in some models and a four wheel drive truck. This inventiveness was not infallible, however, and the 1929 offering of a double-deck bus to carry nearly 70 people, the whole restrained by rear brakes only, is a little hard to comprehend. Perhaps the name the firm gave to another double-decker a couple of years later would have been more appropriate – the Daring!

Along with some other British commercial vehicle manufacturers Thornycroft began to develop its own diesel engines, and by 1933 these were ready for use. During the next few years the company continued to produce new models and update old ones. Forward control was introduced on some vehicles, and a 6x4, the Amazon, for cross-country payloads of up to 6 tons, was launched.

In the years immediately before the war precedence was given to truck production, and when hostilities began the firm was almost ready with military versions of the Amazon, conventional trucks such as the 4-ton Sturdy and a 3-ton 4x4 named the Nubian. These were turned out in their thousands during the following years. Thornycroft's contribution to the war effort is probably best remembered, however, for the destroyers and motor torpedo boats built beside the River Itchen in Southampton.

Old names such as the 8-ton Trusty and Sturdy reappeared immediately after the war and a 15-ton eight-wheeler variant of the Trusty was put into production during 1946. Two years later the commercial vehicle side of the business was given the name Transport Equipment (Thornycroft) Ltd in order to avoid confusion with the much larger shipbuilding business.

In 1950 the fabulous 85-ton Mighty Antar made its appearance. Originally intended for oilfield and pipeline work it was also found to be a very fine tank transporter. Shortly after came the Sturdy Star and smaller Nippy Star, followed by a six-wheeled Nubian derivative and the even larger Big Ben.

The Star models were superseded during 1957 by

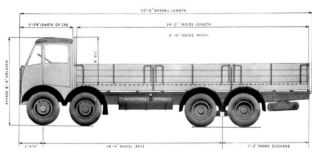

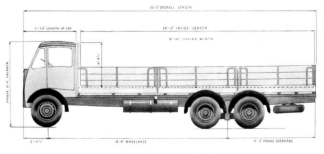

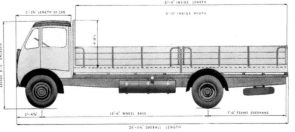

The Trusty class were powered by Thornycroft's own NR6/MV engine. A six-cylinder long-stroke diesel of 104.8 x 152.4mm bore and stroke, its capacity was 7.88 litres and it produced 100bhp at 1750rpm.

The 1951 brochure offered the option, for the Trusty range, of normal-control and left-hand drive for export. There was also, in addition to the chassis configurations shown on the previous page, a tractor version with 9ft 6in wheelbase. All had a five-speed gearbox and air brakes.

The Big Ben brochure (opposite) of 1956 illustrated examples of a 20-ton machinery transporter for the Middle East with insulated cab and also a specialised 'Service' type tractor.

The rear bogie of "Trusty" 6×4 and 8×4 chassis showing spring anchorage and torque arm.

1. TELESCOPIC STEERING WHEEL ALLOWING 3-in. ADJUSTMENT
2. 100 B.H.P. DIRECT INJECTION OIL ENGINE
3. MULTIPLE PULL RATCHET TYPE HAND BRAKE
4. 5-SPEED GEARBOX WITH DOG ENGAGEMENT FOR 3rd, 4th & 5th GEARS
5. THORNYCROFT PATENT TYRE INFLATION DEVICE
6. 40-GALLON FUEL TANK
7. AIR PRESSURE BRAKES OPERATING ON ALL ROAD WHEELS
8. FLEXIBLY-MOUNTED INTERMEDIATE BEARING
9. THIRD DIFFERENTIAL IN FOREMOST BOGIE AXLE
10. 1½-in. BRAKE WITH REINFORCED CONSTRUCTION AT BOGIE
11. DRIVING AND BRAKING TORQUES TRANSMITTED THROUGH A RADIUS ARM COUPLED TO THE CENTRE CROSS TUBE
12. WIND-UP CABLE-TYPE SPARE WHEEL CARRIER

Swift and Swiftsures types, and a little while later a four-wheeler named the Mastiff was brought out.

During 1961 the company was acquired by AEC, the two firms being known as Associated Commercial Vehicles Ltd. Thornycroft products and identity began to be trimmed down. This process was accelerated when ACV was taken over by Leyland Motors a year later. The once proud firm of Thornycroft, or the commercial vehicle portion thereof, found itself a bit-part player in the whole sorrowful Leyland saga which was to be played out over the last part of the 20th century. The Thornycroft name continued to head various products within the group, the last to be brought to the market being a thinly-disguised Aveling-Barford dump truck, but by 1977 even that had disappeared.

THORNYCROFT "BIG BEN"

**For gross laden weights of
47,040 lbs. (21,340 kgs.) solo**
or
89,600 lbs. (40,640 kgs.) with full trailer or semi-trailer

VULCAN

Diesel-powered Vulcans used the 4.73-litre Perkins P6 in conjunction with a four-speed gearbox; an Eaton two-speed axle could be fitted as an extra.

For the first dozen years of its existence the Vulcan company of Southport in Lancashire was exclusively a manufacturer of motor cars, and it was only in 1914 that it began to turn out commercials. Initially Vulcan produced but one model, of 30cwt capacity, which was to see the company through the war years and a bit beyond. A brief liaison with a consortium of car manufacturers which included such makes as Swift and Bean did Vulcan very little good, financially or otherwise, but having disassociated itself from this the company entered the 1920s full of hope and some good ideas. Besides normal small to medium size trucks it also came up with forward-thinking four-wheel drives and half-tracks intended for the military.

Fresh management was appointed during 1928 who, in an attempt to guide the company on to a sounder financial footing, made the decision to cease the manufacture of cars and concentrate solely on commercials. Thereafter a fresh spate of inventiveness was embarked upon which was also to encompass buses, but it was all to no avail and by 1931 Vulcan had gone into liquidation. Under receivership the company was kept going over the next few years, even

LEFT OR RIGHT HAND CONTROL
DIESEL ENGINED 5/6 TON

FREIGHTER OR LIGHT
PASSENGER CHASSIS

Types 6PF, PPF, & 9PFA

VULCAN MOTORS LTD. MAIDSTONE. KENT.

Vulcan Type 6VF Cab—Engine Accessibility Detachable Wing Removed :— Providing space 2' 9" × 11" for engine adjustment.

Although this is the cab of a 6VF with petrol engine, vehicles with the Perkins diesel had exactly the same construction.